THE *Extraordinary* Parents
OF *St. Thérèse of Lisieux*

Sts. Louis and Zélie Martin

By Hélène Mongin

Translated by Marsha Daigle-Williamson, Ph.D.

Nihil Obstat
Paris, September 13, 2008
M. Dupuy

Imprimatur
Paris, September 13, 2008
M. Vidal

© Éditions de l'Emmanuel, 2008, 2015
89 bd Auguste Blanqui, 75013 Paris
www.editions-emmanuel.com

English-language copyright © Our Sunday Visitor Publishing Division. Published 2015.

20 19 18 17 16 15   1 2 3 4 5 6 7 8 9

Our Sunday Visitor Publishing Division, Our Sunday Visitor, Inc., 200 Noll Plaza, Huntington, IN 46750; 1-800-348-2440

ISBN: 978-1-61278-964-4 (Inventory No. T1728)
eISBN: 978-1-61278-970-5
LCCN: 2015947317

Cover design: Lindsey Riesen
Cover art: © Office Central de Lisieux, Carmel de Lisieux, Lisieux sanctuary
Interior design: Dianne Nelson

PRINTED IN THE UNITED STATES OF AMERICA

To Jean-Paul and Morina,
Stéphane and Julie,
Patrick and Joséphine,
the Martins of tomorrow

TABLE OF CONTENTS

WE, THE ORDINARY PEOPLE

God calls some people and sets them apart. But there are people he leaves in the crowd, those that he does not "withdraw from the world."

These are people who do ordinary work, who have an ordinary family, or who are ordinary single people. These are people with ordinary sicknesses and ordinary sorrows. They live in ordinary houses and wear ordinary clothes. They are people with ordinary lives—people that we meet on any street. . . .

As people on ordinary streets, we believe with our whole hearts that the street, the world that God has placed us in, is the place of our holiness.

It doesn't matter what work we do, whether we are holding a broom or a pen, speaking or being silent, repairing things or giving a lecture, taking care of a sick person, or typing on a computer.

All of that is only the shell of a splendid reality—the encounter of the soul with God, renewed each moment, growing in grace each minute, always becoming lovelier for God.

Is the doorbell ringing? Quick, let's open the door. God is coming to love us. Need information? Here it is. . . . God is coming to love us. Is it time to eat? Let's sit down to eat because God is coming to love us.

Let's let him do it.

Madeleine Delbrêl
We, the Ordinary People of the Streets
(*Nous autres, gens des rues* [1971])

Abbreviations

CF Louis et Zélie Martin, *Correspondance familiale, 1863–1885*, Editions du Cerf, 2004.

HF Father Stéphane-Joseph Piat, O.F.M., *Histoire d'une famille*, Tequi, 1997.

LT *Lettres de Thérèse de L'Enfant-Jésus*

PN *Poésies de Thérèse de L'Enfant-Jésus*

(The numbering of the letters and the poems is from the centenary edition of *Oeuvres complètes* published in 1992.)

Preface

Since their beatification on October 19, 2008, Louis and Zélie Martin, the parents of Thérèse of Lisieux, are becoming known for their originality and authenticity. We are struck by their vitality, their modernity, and their dynamism. They are connected to us by their life experience: their youth, their growth as a couple, their joy at the birth of children, their relationship with their children, changes within the family, sickness, the death of a spouse—all of it the antithesis of any idealized image.

More and more people are discovering about them what their daughter Thérèse so rightly described about people in heaven: "The Blessed have great compassion for our sufferings; they remember that being fragile and mortal like us, they made the same mistakes and fought the same battles, and their fraternal tenderness toward us becomes even greater than it was on earth. That is why they do not stop protecting us and praying for us."[1]

In this book, Hélène Mongin gives us a new, affectionate, and intensive look at the Martins. We can perhaps imagine that one of the Martin daughters would have liked to speak to us this way about her parents. An enthusiastic Hélène has let Thérèse's parents into her life after having been enthralled with their daughter. She guides us now to a relationship with Louis and Zélie, to loving them, to giving them a place in our lives . . . and invites us to follow them.

Monsignor Bernard Lagoutte
Rector Emeritus
Shrine of Lisieux

---

[1] *LT* 263, August 10, 1897.

Introduction

The canonization of Louis and Zélie is a historic event because, for the first time in its history, the Church is canonizing a married couple together. And not just any couple. They are the parents of Thérèse of the Child Jesus, "the greatest saint in modern times," according to Pope Pius XI.

Louis and Zélie have not been canonized because of their daughter, however. She, of course, revealed their faces to her readers. And in other respects this saying of Christ—"you will know them by their fruits" (see Mt 7:17-20)—can be applied to Thérèse and her parents, but her role ends there. It is the very holiness of Louis and Zélie themselves that the Church is recognizing in their prophetic holiness. Their example shows us in fact that holiness, far from being an ideal reserved for elite souls, consecrated souls, or martyrs, is a choice and a grace offered to everyone.

And so the Church wants to highlight a holy family in our age and offer a hopeful response to violent attacks on the nuclear family today.

Louis and Zélie, despite the century that separates us, had lives that are surprisingly similar to those of our contemporaries. Both of them were working while they raised their children, they were always busy, they knew the joys and sorrows of ordinary families, and they died of illnesses that are familiar to us: breast cancer for Zélie and arteriosclerosis for Louis, an illness that affected his brain and put him in a psychiatric hospital for three years. The holiness of the Martin spouses doesn't come from any events themselves but from the manner in which they lived. In every aspect of their lives they had only one source and one goal:

God's love. This heart orientation, far from making them un-earthly, made their ordinary lives an adventure of love in which they raised up their family, their neighbors, their friends, their employees, and even the whole Church.

I hope that the reader will share the joy I had in studying the lives of Louis and Zélie. In doing so, I made use of several documents that I recommend to those who wish to know more about the Martin couple:

— *Correspondance familiale (1863-1885)*, [*Family Correspondence from 1863 to 1885*] (Paris: Éditions du Cerf, 2004), which contains 217 letters from Zélie, most of which were sent to her brother and sister-in-law in Lisieux from 1863 until her death in 1877. She is the family letter writer since Louis didn't like to write. All through this period, it's not surprising that she takes center stage in the story since the sources for her are much more abundant. These lively letters, written in a spirit of freedom and humor, allow us to know Zélie and her family intimately. In that same book there are fifteen letters by Louis, most of them written after the death of his wife, which show him to be a tender man of depth focused on God.

— *Histoire d'une famille* [*The Story of a Family*], by Father Stéphane-Joseph Piat, O.F.M. (1946; repr. ed., Paris: Téqui, 1997). This is the authorized biography of the family; daughter Céline Martin stated everything in it was true. It first appeared in 1946, so it's written in a bit of an outdated style, but it's complete and well documented.

— *Zélie Martin* and *Louis Martin*, by Dr. Robert Cadéot (François-Xavier de Guibert, 1996), two excellent biographies based on the testimony of Céline about her parents and on excellent historical research. Unfortunately, both are currently out of print.

— *Zélie et Louis Martin, les saints de l'escalier*, by Henri and Alice Quantin (Ed. du Cerf, 2004). Without agreeing with all of their analyses, I have to thank them for the brilliant way in which they demonstrated the incoherence of the base accusations made against Louis and Zélie by authors who do not deserve to be mentioned. This allowed me not to have deal with the same painful polemic.

— *La mère de sainte Thérèse de l'Enfant-Jésus* and *Le père de sainte Thérèse de l'Enfant-Jésus*, both written by Céline Martin (Carmel of Lisieux, 1953-1954).

— *Les Oeuvres complètes* (Ed. du Cerf, 1992), by Thérèse de l'Enfant-Jésus, which is still the best source about Louis.

— Numerous editions of *Thérèse de Lisieux* and of *Vie thérésienne*, well-documented journals published by the Pèlerinage Sainte Thérèse de Lisieux.

— The website www.archives-carmel-lisieux.fr is a gold mine for photos, texts, and documents on Thérèse, and also on her whole family.

We could summarize the history that follows according to what we hear in fairy tales: "They lived happily and had many children"—but they did so in the shadow of the cross. And now we enter intimately into a very real and engaging family to see the faces of Louis and Zélie, so human but holy.

Chapter 1

YOUTH OR THE DESIRE FOR GOD

On July 13, 1858, Louis Martin married Zélie Guérin in the beautiful Notre-Dame d'Alençon Church. He was thirty-four and she was twenty-six. They had known each other for three months, but they didn't doubt for a minute that this marriage was God's will. This was not the vocation that these two fervent hearts had aspired to in their youth, however. The road that brought them to each other demonstrates how much "God writes straight with crooked lines."

Louis was born on August 22, 1823, in Bordeaux. His father, Pierre-François Martin, was a captain in the French army who had participated in the Napoleonic wars and lived in various garrisons in Bordeaux, Avignon, and Strasbourg. In 1818, Pierre-François married Fanny Boureau, the daughter of one of his military friends, and supplied the dowry that she could not furnish. The offspring of this couple included Louis as well as four brothers and sisters (who all died young).

His parents' faith was vibrant. One day when the soldiers asked Captain Martin why he stayed on his knees so long during Mass, he answered, "It is because I believe." His relatives were equally taken by the manner in which he recited the Our Father. As for Fanny, she was a woman of prayer, as this extract from a letter sent to her son shows: "How often I think of you when my soul, lifted up to God, follows the impulse of my heart right to the foot of God's throne! There I pray with all the fervor of my soul."[2] Louis was thus presented the Catholic faith from a very early age.

We know little about his early years. From garrison to garrison, those years were regulated by the military life that gave Louis his penchant for discipline and travel. In 1830 Captain Martin retired and went to live in his native region of Normandy in the city of Alençon. Louis didn't attend secondary school but received enough education to demonstrate clear intelligence and discernment, especially in literature. He could have chosen a military career like his father; however, the French army had lost its luster since the end of the Napoleonic era. Louis had less of a penchant for adventure and more of an inclination toward interiority.

Discovering the delicate and detailed craft of watchmaking after visiting an uncle in that profession in Rennes, he fell in love with both watchmaking and Brittany. He lived there in 1842 and 1843, learning the basics of that craft while at the same time immersing himself in reading the great authors. He copied numerous texts in notebooks and from these we know that he particularly liked the Romantics, with a preference for François-René Châteaubriand, and he also appreciated the writings of Jacques-Bénigne Bossuet, François Fénelon, and similar authors.

Louis's literary tastes reveal an important character trait: he was sensitive to beauty whether in literature or in the landscapes of Brittany. Often, while walking in the countryside, he would stop to weep before the magnificent beauty of creation. Although romantic sensibility was common for this era, Louis's

---

[2] Father Stéphane-Joseph Piat, O.F.M., *Histoire d'une famille* [*The Story of a Family*] (1946; repr ed., Paris: Téqui, 1997), p. 13. Future references to this work will be indicated by *HF* and page number.

sensibility was different insofar as he always discovered the Creator in whatever he was contemplating. Few things made him so happy as taking his pilgrim's staff and walking around magnificent places while praying.

He did that for the first time in September 1843 when he crossed the Swiss Alps on foot and discovered the dream of his youth: the Grand Saint Bernard Monastery. The famous building is set at over 8,000 feet, and here the Canons of Saint Augustine divided their time between contemplation and mountain rescues. Prayer, beauty, heroism—this is what appealed to his young soul in love with the absolute.

For two years, Louis let the desire to enter this order mature in him while he continued his apprenticeship training in watchmaking in Strasbourg. They were good years. He made wonderful friends with whom he shared a joyful and prayerful youth. But he put an end to this period in 1845, wanting to return to the Grand Saint Bernard Monastery to answer what he felt was a call from the Lord. But then a disappointment occurred. The abbot, who was initially enthusiastic about this fervent and level-headed young man, had reservations when he learned that Louis had not attended secondary school. To enter the monastery, young men needed to know Latin. He invited Louis to return after he went back to school and finished his studies. Louis returned to Alençon, and for more than a year he plunged into his books and took courses in Latin. An illness interrupted his efforts, however. Louis discerned a sign from Providence in that circumstance, and with a heavy heart he set aside his aspirations for monastic life.

He then decided to finish his training as a watchmaker in Paris. He was severely tested by Parisian life, experiencing numerous temptations: examples of dissolute life, an invitation to join a secret society, the influence of liberal Voltairean thinking, difficulty in keeping a prayer life in the hustle and bustle of the capital . . . According to his own testimony, it took a lot of courage for him to emerge victorious. From this time on, he relied not on his own strength but on God's strength for his courage. The young Louis redoubled his prayer and entrusted himself to the Blessed Virgin in the sanctuary of the Basilica of Notre-Dame des Victoires, a church he always particularly liked.

Like gold tested in the crucible, Louis emerged purified from his time in the capital and relied on that experience for the rest of his life. He knew the temptations that life could bring and never stopped exposing them and encouraging his relatives not to fall into them.

Comforted by having a career well in hand, he returned to Alençon and set up a watchmaker's shop on Rue du Pont-Neuf and later added a jewelry shop to it. Louis was twenty-seven years old, and the next eight years his life unfolded peacefully in prayer, work, reading, and recreation. Because of his cheerful, agreeable, and pensive character, he quickly made friends whom he regularly joined in the Vital Romet Club, a small group named after its founder (who was a great friend of Louis)—the members played billiards as well as studied their faith. He spent equally long hours at his favorite pastime, fishing.

In 1857 he bought a small property known as the Pavilion. It included an octagonal tower that he furnished simply, decorating its walls, as they do in monasteries, with pious sentences that revealed his spirituality: "God sees me"; "Eternity approaches and we do not consider it"; "Blessed are those who keep the commandments of the Lord." He often went there to read and pray.[3]

Father Stéphane-Joseph Piat gives us a wonderful description of Louis during this period: He was "tall in stature, with the bearing of an officer, a pleasing physiognomy, a high, wide fore-

---

[3] People can visit the Pavilion in Alençon, and no place reveals Louis's soul better to a pilgrim than this place.

head, fair complexion, a pleasant face framed by chestnut hair, and a soft, deep light in his hazel eyes. He looked like both a gentleman and a mystic and didn't fail to make an impression."[4] Nor did he fail to attract the attention of the young girls in the city. But Louis categorically rejected any idea of marriage—he was still grieving over his unfulfilled desire for a monastic vocation. He even started studying Latin regularly again. More and more the life of this quiet young man of thirty-four approximated a quasi-monastic life in the world. But his mother was keeping her eye out. It was unthinkable for Fanny Martin to see her cherished son end up as a bachelor. She sought at all costs to see him married, and she ended up finding the rare pearl.

Marie-Azélie Guérin, called Zélie, was born on December 23, 1831, in Saint-Denis-sur-Sarthon in the Department of Orne. Similar to the Martin father, her father was a military man involved in the Napoleonic Wars who decided to retire in Alençon. His retirement pension was meager, so the family had to count every penny; Zélie never even had a doll. The family atmosphere didn't seem to be the happiest. The father, Isidore Guérin, was a good but surly man, and his wife, Louise-Jeanne, was a woman with little affection who often merged faith and rigid moralism. Zélie would say of her childhood that it was as "sad as a shroud" and that because of her mother's severity "my heart suffered a lot."[5]

Zélie didn't flourish any better on the physical level than she had on the emotional level. From the age of seven to twelve, she was continually ill and spent her adolescence tormented by

---

[4] *HF*, p. 25.

[5] *Correspondance familiale* (1863-1885) [*Family Correspondence from 1863 to 1885*] (Paris: Éditions du Cerf, 2004), Letter 15. Future citations from this text will be listed as *CF* with the letter number.

migraine headaches. This did not, however, prevent her from receiving a good education with the Sisters of Perpetual Adoration. Fortunately, she had a brother and a sister who played major
roles in her life: Marie-Louise, called Élise, the older sister, her
confidant and her support, who was as close to her as a twin;
and Isidore, who was ten years younger and whom she loved as
a mother would.

The Guérin family had also come from a strong Catholic
tradition. They liked to tell the adventures of their great-uncle
Guillaume who was a priest during the French Revolution.
Sought out by the "Blues,"[6] he went into hiding. One day, when
he was bringing the Eucharist to a family, he was attacked by a
band of rogues. He placed the Blessed Sacrament down on a pile
of rocks, saying, "God, take care of yourself while I take care of
these guys," and threw his assailants into the nearby swamp. Another time he owed his life to the presence of mind of Zélie's father who, when he was just a child, made believe he was playing
on the chest in which his uncle was hiding from the soldiers. At
the Guérin home, faith was rooted in their hearts even if it was
tainted by the rigorous Jansenism that was rampant at that time.

Because of her sad childhood, Zélie could have been just
an anxious, hypersensitive young woman full of scruples and
lacking in self-confidence. She was actually all of those things,
but from her youth she also demonstrated St. Paul's axiom that
"when I am weak, then I am strong" (2 Cor 12:10). Doubting her
own capabilities, Zélie early on relied on God, knowing that his
strength would never fail. Her relationship with him was so profound that before the age of twenty she believed she was called
to religious life. As was the case for Louis, her choice of which

---

[6] The "Blues," named for the color of their uniforms, were the troops sup-
porting the new republic that fought against the peasants during the
French Revolution.

convent to join revealed her generous personality: Zélie wanted
to become part of the Daughters of Charity of St. Vincent de
Paul, apostolic sisters who combine a life of prayer and active
service to the poor. But again, the Lord, who knows the hearts of
his children so well, blocked her path. The superior clearly said
that she didn't believe Zélie had that vocation. For Zélie it was a
hard blow, but she wasn't one to wallow in her unhappiness. She
decided to be trained in a profession.

During her years of study she had learned the basics of the
noble craft of lace-making in Alençon. The Arachnean lace that
Napoleon admired required intensive manual dexterity and delicacy. Zélie decided to pursue this profession and excelled at it.
At first she worked in a factory in Alençon, but she attracted
the persistent attentions of a member of the personnel so she
decided to quit that job. On December 8, 1851, the feast of the
Immaculate Conception, while she was working in her room, she
heard an inner voice clearly say, "You are to make Alençon lace."
She immediately talked to her sister, Élise, who encouraged her
and promised her support.

Both of them then launched an enterprise that was more
than bold, as she admitted later: "How did we—without any
monetary resources to speak of and without any understanding
of business—end up doing well and finding establishments in
Paris who would trust our work? Yet that is what happened in a
very short time because we started working the very next day."[7]
She wasn't even twenty years old. Zélie established herself as a
maker of Alençon-style lace and as the proprietor of that business.

Father Piat gives us another wonderful description, this time
of Zélie:

---

[7] *HF*, p. 29.

Somewhat shorter than average, a very pretty and inno-
cent face, brown hair in a simple style, a long well-shaped
nose, dark eyes glowing with decision that occasionally
had a shadow of melancholy, she was an attractive young
woman. Everything about her was vivacious, refined, and
amiable. With a lively and refined spirit, good common
sense, great character, and above all an intrepid faith, this
was an above-average woman who could draw people's
attention.[8]

As the years went by, divided between prayer and work, she
bonded even more with her sister in the midst of the trials of
starting up a business and the trial of an opposite vocation for
Élise. Élise had been interested in cloistered life but had run into
obstacle after obstacle because of health issues and attacks of
scrupulosity. On April 7, 1858, she finally landed at the doorstep
of the Visitation Monastery in Le Mans with the radical desire
of becoming a saint. For Zélie the separation was heart-rending.
At that time she could barely stand to be separated from her
sister even for an afternoon. "What will you do when I am not
here any more?" her sister had asked her.[9] Zélie said she would
leave too. And that is what she did three months after her sister
entered the convent. She went in a new direction . . . to marry
Louis.

Louis's mother, Fanny Martin, was taking some lessons in lace-
making in Alençon and met Zélie, whom she immediately appreciated; with her solid maternal instinct, she saw in her an ideal
daughter-in-law. She talked about her to Louis, doubtless presenting more arguments to him about her piety than her beauty.

---

[8] *HF*, p. 32.
[9] *CF* 190.

Louis's resistance was overcome and he was open to meeting Zélie.

Zélie didn't have an attentive mother to counsel her, but she had the Holy Spirit: Zélie crossed paths by chance with Louis for the first time on a bridge. Not only did his attractive appearance vividly impress her, but again an inner voice confirmed to her, "This is the one I have prepared for you." Young people in the process of discernment could envy such clarity. But let's not forget that Zélie, like Louis, had done all she could to find her vocation and had gone through deserts for it. She also had her heart open enough to hear the voice of the Holy Spirit in this way. The Spirit didn't have to reveal the name of "the promised one" since Fanny Martin would take care of that a few days later.

The two young people met in April 1858 and quickly grew fond of each other, rapidly establishing a rapport. They got engaged, and with the consent of the priest who prepared them for marriage they decided to get married on July 13.

Nine children were born from this union. Louis and Zélie raised them while continuing in their watchmaking and lacemaking professions. Five daughters were born who lived: Marie in 1860, Pauline in 1861, Léonie in 1863, Céline in 1869, and Thérèse in 1873. Four little "angels" left early for heaven: Hélène in 1870 (at the age of 5), Joseph in 1866, Jean-Baptiste-Joseph in 1867, and their first daughter named Thérèse, in 1870.

Chapter 2

A MARRIAGE OF LOVE

W hat kind of couple were Louis and Zélie? Let's look at their foundation in God as a couple on July 13, 1858.

They were married at the odd hour of midnight, a local tradition. Louis gave his wife a beautiful medallion representing Tobit and Sarah, the biblical couple. Tobit, during the night of his wedding, had prayed: "O Lord, I am not taking this sister of mine because of lust, but with sincerity. Grant that I may find mercy and may grow old together with her" (Tb 8:7).

Fifteen years later Zélie would tell her daughter Pauline the story of her first day of marriage, which wasn't a typical first day for a young couple. After going to the convent to present her husband to her sister (now Sister Marie-Dosithée), she spent the day in tears. Seeing her sister as a nun awoke the suffering of their separation and stirred up her regret at the loss of a consecrated life, especially since she had just now committed to live "in the world" because of her marriage. But there is also a more delicate shock to recount: the prior evening, Louis had to explain to her "the things of life," as they used to say for modesty's sake—that is to say, the facts about sexuality, which Zélie had been perfectly ignorant of. It's an ignorance we find astounding in our age, but it was quite common at that time.

One can easily imagine Zélie's difficulty in absorbing these sudden revelations, a difficulty which could also explain her tears the following day. This is the point at which Louis—with an uncommon sensitivity—proposed that they live as brother and sister. The reasons for this proposition were not only the respect he had for his wife but also his aspiration to be a saint. He had studied the issue of virginity in marriage and his notebooks contain several texts on the validity of marriages that are not consummated, with Mary and Joseph being the perfect example. For these young people who had dreamed of consecrating themselves to God at a time when the perfection of virginity was highly praised by the Church, this seemed to be the solution: to marry, but to live in the marriage like religious.

We can smile at this plan today, but we need to understand the generosity and respect for the other that underlies it. Speaking in euphemistic words about this choice when she told Pauline about her first day of marriage, Zélie commented: "Your father understood me and comforted me the best he could since he had inclinations that were similar to mine. I believe our mutual affection was even more increased through this, and we were always united in our feelings."[10] Louis and Zélie had an experience of chastity similar to that of young people today who are chaste before marriage, and they testify by what followed to the solidity that such a choice produced in them as a couple. During this period, Zélie wrote to her sister how happy she was. They lived as brother and sister for ten months, meanwhile opening themselves up to life by taking in for a time a small boy that a recently widowed and overwhelmed father had entrusted to them. It was a time of maturation for them as a couple and of better understanding their vocation.

Little by little, Louis and Zélie discovered that their marriage—far from being a replacement by God for the failure of their plans to consecrate themselves—was their true calling, to be lived out fully. When their confessor invited them to set a

---

[10] *CF* 192.

time to end their abstinence, they were ready to accept it. The arrival of children confirmed them even more in their vocation: "When we had our children, our ideas changed a bit; we lived only for them; they were all our joy, and we never found our joy except in them. Nothing was too costly for us to do for them; the world was no longer a burden."[11] The one who would exclaim that she was "made to have children" maintained a great respect, as did her husband, for religious life but had no regrets. "Oh! I do not regret getting married," she told her brother.[12]

God oriented their desire for holiness toward the state in life in which they would blossom the most: marriage, and in particular parenthood. Louis and Zélie recognized God's call to have many children and—in their lovely phrase—"to raise them for heaven."[13] Contrary to their initial ideas, it was not in spite of marriage but in and through marriage that they were to become holy.

The couple they became was based on a solid friendship full of tenderness and cooperation that the years only served to deepen. After five years of marriage, Zélie wrote: "I am still very happy with him; he makes life very pleasant. My husband is a holy man, and I wish that all women could have such husbands."[14] Whenever Zélie talked to someone about her husband, she couldn't help always adding the same adjective, "my *good* Louis." It's a small word, but it sheds a lot of light on their relationship. More than friendship, however, one can see the enormous place they had in each other's hearts through the feeling of loss they experienced when they were occasionally separated. The letters they

---

[11] Ibid.
[12] *CF* 13.
[13] *CF* 192.
[14] *CF* 1.

wrote to each other at those times demonstrated all the vibrancy
of a love full of tenderness. Away on a trip with the children to
visit her brother and his wife, Zélie wrote:

> The children are delighted, and if the weather were good
> they would be at the height of happiness. But as for me,
> I find relaxation difficult! None of all that interests me! I
> am absolutely like a fish out of water that is not in its ele-
> ment and must perish! If my trip were to be prolonged,
> it would have that same effect for me. I'm uncomfortable
> and out of sorts, which affects my body and I'm almost
> sick because of it. Meanwhile, I try to reason with myself
> and rally from the sickness. I follow you in spirit all day
> long; I say to myself, "He is doing this or that right now."
> I am longing to be near you, my dear Louis. I love you
> with all my heart, and my affection for you is increasing
> because I am deprived of your presence; it would be im-
> possible for me to live apart from you. . . . I embrace you
> and I love you."[15]

Does this sound like the excitement of a young married
woman in love? Not in this case. This letter was written after fifteen years of marriage. Louis had become Zélie's "element." And
when Louis in turn had to leave home for business, he wrote
with his characteristic thoughtfulness:

> My dear Friend, I cannot come back to Alençon until
> Monday. The time seems long to me, and I'm eager to be
> near you. I don't need to tell you that your letter brought
> me great pleasure, except that I see you're tiring yourself
> out too much. So I recommend calm and moderation,

---

[15] *CF* 108.

especially in your work. I have a few orders from the Lyons Company. Once again, don't worry so much; we will end up, with God's help, at having a nice little business. I was happy to receive communion at Notre-Dame des Victoires, which is like a little earthly paradise. I also lit a candle there for the whole family. I embrace you with all my heart while I await the joy of being reunited to you. I hope that Marie and Pauline are being very good! Your husband and true friend, who loves you for life.[16]

These rare letters reveal a cooperation that withstood the years and the minor difficulties that we can sometimes read between the lines. "When you receive this letter, I will be busy rearranging your work bench, so don't get mad," Zélie once wrote. "I will lose nothing, not an old square piece, not the end of a spring, nothing. And then it will be clean all over! You will not be able to say, 'You only shifted the dust around' because there will not be any. . . . I embrace you with all my heart; I am so happy today at the thought of seeing you again that I cannot work. Your wife, who loves you more than her own life."[17] The last words Zélie ever wrote to Louis were, "I am all yours."[18]

Her letters and the testimony of her daughters let us see the kind of wife she was: joyful, lively, tender, open to everyone, confident of her husband, and full of humor, with a special gift for making fun of herself. The contrast is striking in terms of how she perceived herself as anguished, depressed, and far from holy. Anguish was present throughout her whole life, and she affirmed at times it was a veritable torment for her. When trials became

---

[16] *CF* 2.
[17] *CF* 46.
[18] *CF* 208.

too heavy, she let herself be overcome by what she called "dark thoughts," but more and more her faith and the supportive presence of Louis helped her to overcome her suffering.

Zélie was a strong and holy woman not because she was without fears and weaknesses, but because despite them she gave of herself generously to others and to God, with a trust that was always wholehearted. Her great sensitivity gave her an exquisite discernment about others. Moreover, she was a woman of action. She worked for her family and in her business without letup and without taking time to coddle herself. Sensing within the need to give herself permanently, she responded with so much generosity that she died with her needle in her hand, so to speak, without ever having the least bit of rest.

Céline described her mother during the process of beatification of Thérèse as being gifted with a superior intelligence and extraordinary energy. Zélie described herself, without realizing it, when she wanted to instruct her brother on a choice for a good wife: "The main thing is to look for a good woman who is domestic, who is not afraid to get her hands dirty when she works, who does not spend time on her appearance except for what is necessary, and who knows how to raise children to work and to be holy."[19] Of course, all this advice lacks any romanticism. Louis and Zélie didn't lack a romantic side, but at a time when marriages of love were the exception, Zélie's advice demonstrates the common sense of a woman from Normandy. Zélie was a good wife for Louis, and he was very complimentary of her.

Calm and thoughtful, he assumed the responsibility for the family and supported his wife with great tenderness. People often said that he was a gentle man, at times implying that he was a bit soft, but he was far from being soft, and he was just as hardworking as his wife. His extreme gentleness at the end of

---

[19] *CF* 10.

his life—so striking to those around him—was acquired more by a faithful practice of charity than by any innate characteristic of his. Thérèse would say that, following the example of St. Francis de Sales, he had managed to master his natural vivacity to the point that he seemed to have the sweetest nature in the world.

Louis took concern for others no less than Zélie did. He was above all a man of great uprightness, tolerating neither injustice nor hypocrisy. His determined temperament was fully in play when it was a question of fighting for spiritual causes or against inequities. Despite not liking to write, he pestered officials with his letters to help a needy man be admitted into a home for the elderly. Zélie's goodness softened his sharp angles, inspiring him by her example to have more mercy toward an undeserving worker or stopping him from getting too wrapped up in solitude. In addition to sharing the same native milieu, similar social ideas, generous hearts, and energy put to good use, Louis and Zélie had in common a preference for work that required finesse and patience, and, above all, they both had a thirst for God.

According to the unanimous testimony of their daughters and their family letters, the communication between the spouses was deep and real. They spoke frankly to each other and often knew what the other was thinking: "He didn't need to say it; I knew very well what he thought."[20] Louis didn't hesitate to tell his wife about his past temptations in Paris so that his story could be of help to her brother, Isidore, when he went to Paris to study. They likewise spoke about a thousand and one things concerning daily life and their children's adventures. Their favorite topic of conversation was faith, and they liked to read the lives of the saints together and discuss them, sharing their impressions and edifying each other.

---

[20] *CF* 19.

They also knew how to respect quiet times and give each other space to accommodate their differences: Louis would regularly go to the Pavilion property or leave on pilgrimage. Zélie in turn would take time to write letters to her brother and sister or to attend devotional meetings.

In terms of daily worries, large or small, they handled them together. Louis often reassured Zélie, who ever since her childhood had a propensity to worry. "Once again, do not torment yourself so much," he would say. At the end of her life she wrote about her husband, "He was always my consoler and my support."[21] Zélie herself was also a support for him—for example, when Louis was concerned about her health: "I have seen my husband often torment himself on this issue for my sake, while I stayed very calm. I would say to him, 'Don't be afraid, God is with us.'"[22] When worries entered the household, it was she, as the heart of that home, who cheered everybody up. Louis and Zélie were pillars for each other in a wonderfully harmonious way.

Of course, the couple had frictions that created small, unforeseen annoyances. Louis, for example, despite being a seasoned traveler, forgot one day to get off the train with his daughters when they were coming back to Alençon from Lisieux, which left his wife waiting eagerly at home with the uneaten meal that she had spent the morning preparing. Once the initial annoyance was over, she quickly laughed about it when she wrote about the incident to Isidore. Although they sometimes argued, it didn't poison their relationship, as seen in the following anecdote. Pauline, who was seven years old at the time, approached her mother after hearing voices raised and asked if that was what people meant by "getting along poorly together." Zélie burst out laughing and quickly told her husband who also laughed. From that time on Pauline's inquiry became a family joke.

---

[21] *CF* 192.
[22] *CF* 65.

As with many couples, the major topic of disagreement concerned the children. Although Louis and Zélie were perfectly in accord on the general topic of education for their children, their opinions could diverge when it came to minor decisions. When Zélie took Céline to Lisieux with her when she was a baby, Louis thought it was madness. He himself sent Marie off to boarding school when she was sick, against Zélie's advice (which caused an outbreak of measles throughout the whole school). Zélie's accounts carry no resentment about all that and, on the contrary, show a healthy balance.

Louis made most of the decisions, as a man of his time and as a biblical man, so to speak: "Wives, be subject to your husbands, as to the Lord. For the husband is head of the wife as Christ is head of the church. . . . As the Church is subject to Christ, so let wives also be subject in everything to their husbands. Let each one of you love his wife as himself, and let the wife see that she respects her husband" (Eph 5:22-24, 33). The Martins perfectly embodied this model of a Gospel couple, giving it a human face.

Louis didn't exercise his authority in a unilateral manner. He was open to discussion, and even when he didn't adopt his wife's views, he let her do things her own way. As the old saying goes, "What the woman wants is what God wants." That was true in the Martin family as seen in this delightful story that Zélie related to Pauline:

> As for Marie's retreat at the Visitation Monastery, you know how he doesn't like to be separated from any of you, and he had first expressly said that she could not go. I saw that he was adamant about this, so I didn't try to plead her case. I just determined very resolutely to come back to the subject. Last night, Marie was complaining about this issue. I told her, "Let me take care of it; I always get what I want without having to fight. There is

still a month to go and that is enough time to persuade your father ten times over."

I wasn't wrong because hardly an hour afterward when he came home, he started talking to your sister in a friendly way as she was energetically working. I said to myself, "Good, this is the right time.". . . So I brought up the issue. Your father asked Marie, "Do you really want to go on this retreat?" When she said yes, he said, "Ok, then, you can go." And you know he is someone who doesn't like our absences and unplanned expenses, so he was telling me just yesterday, "If I don't want her to go there, she will of course not go. There seems to be no end to all these trips to Le Mans and Lisieux." I agreed with him then, but I had an ulterior motive because for a long time I've known how these things work. When I tell someone, "My husband does not want it," it is because I don't want the thing any more than he does. But when I have a good reason on my side, I know how to help him decide, and I found I had a good reason for wanting Marie to go on the retreat.

It's true that it's an expense, but money is nothing when it comes to the sanctification and perfection of one's soul. Last year, Marie came back to me all transformed with fruit that lasted, but she needs to renew her supply now. Besides, that is also what your father essentially believes and why he yielded so nicely.[23]

Notice that if Zélie can so sweetly "manipulate" her husband it's because they are essentially in agreement deep down. Besides, "manipulate" is the wrong word for a woman who, a few days

---

[23] *CF* 201.

later in writing to her daughter, picked up right where she had left off in her letter: "My dear Pauline, I stopped at that last sentence. Sunday night at 7:00 your father asked me to go out with him, and since I am very obedient, I didn't finish the sentence!"[24] These incidents emphasize Zélie's feminine character, Louis's flexibility, and above all their good mutual understanding.

To understand the life of the Martin couple we need to know about their relatives and their surroundings. Zélie's closest relatives were her brother and sister. Although Louis rarely visited Sister Marie-Dosithée because she lived too far away, he was aware of her influence on his wife. Linked by blood and a deep friendship, the two women were also linked by a genuine spiritual sisterhood: "If you saw the letter I wrote to my sister in Le Mans, you would be jealous because it is five pages long," she wrote teasingly to Isidore. "But I tell her things I do not tell you. She and I share together about the mysterious, angelic world, but I have to talk to you about earthly things."[25]

What a shame that those letters weren't preserved. They've disappeared, along with the letters to her daughters to prepare them for their first Communion that were so admired by the Visitation sisters. The letters that we have from Zélie only show her with a needle and a baby in each arm. But even this depiction reveals her deep interior life, and the major role her sister had on her path. As a confidant to her sorrows as well as joys, Sister Marie-Dosithée knew how to help Zélie discover God's hand, as we shall see. Zélie never undertook any step in her affairs without entrusting it to the prayer of "the saint of Le Mans,"[26] as she called her. This was especially true for family affairs.

---

[24] *CF* 202.

[25] *CF* 12.

[26] *CF* 17.

As for Isidore, he was always the little brother they coddled. Zélie, together with Sister Marie-Dosithée, played a somewhat maternal role in his life. From Le Mans to Alençon, pious advice rained down on Isidore's head. He pretended to mock it, but he appreciated it and ended up following it. In 1866, Isidore married Céline Fournet, a spouse completely along the lines prescribed by his sisters—good, pious, simple, and hardworking. The people in Thérèse's circle said little about this quiet woman, but she was well loved by all the Martins. In 1875, Zélie wrote: "I have a sister-in-law who is incomparably good and sweet. Marie says she can find no faults in her, and I cannot either. . . . I assure you I love her like a sister, and she seems to feel the same way about me. She demonstrates an almost maternal attitude to my children and has given them as much attention as possible."[27] Isidore bought his father-in-law's pharmacy in Lisieux and committed himself more and more to the life of the local church and also supported the Catholic newspaper in Lisieux.

Once Isidore was established in Lisieux, his relationship with Zélie was on a more equal footing. "I have known you for a long time," she wrote to him, "and I know you love me and have a good heart. If I needed you, I am sure you would not let me down. Our friendship is sincere; it does not consist in pretty words, that is true, but it is no less solid and is built on stone. Neither time, nor any person, nor even death will ever destroy it."[28] All the letters she sent him showed this same affection.

Zélie shared in all her brother's sentiments: When he lost a child she cried as though she had lost one of her own. She often wanted to spend a few days at her brother's home in Lisieux—for her, and then for her children, going there was always a holiday. Isidore was also the medical adviser for the family, although he wasn't always happy about that. The family submitted all minor

---

[27] *CF* 138.
[28] *CF* 19.

health problems to him for his judgment, and then heeded it in a trusting manner.

The Martins, for their part, gave whatever help they could to the Guérin family: advice, monetary loans, and clients sent his way. The distance between the families was difficult to overcome, especially because each family was working and had babies, but the bond between them was nourished by frequent mail and always remained strong. The letters from Lisieux were read, reread, and passed around the family. And Zélie at times didn't hesitate to get up at 4:30 a.m. to answer them. This bond was so strong for Zélie that in 1875 she wrote about Isidore and his family: "If I did not have a home and children here, I would live only for them, and I would give them all the money I earned. But since I cannot do that, God will provide."[29]

Louis and Zélie's life together evolved in the heart of the parish and the different Catholic circles where they visited with their few but close friends. The Romet, Maudelonde, Boul, and Leriche families and Mrs. Leconte regularly visited them on Rue du Pont-Neuf and, after 1871, at 34 Rue Saint-Blaise. Their second home—a small, charming, middle-class house facing the prefecture that can still be visited today—would be Thérèse's first home and Zélie's last. Zélie commented: "We are wonderfully settled in here. My husband has set up everything in a way that would please me."[30]

As for worldly outings, they had few. Soon after their marriage, the young couple preferred intimate meetings instead of shallow balls at big parties. Zélie depicted the ridiculousness of high society when writing about an upcoming ball: "I know many young women who have their heads on backwards. There are some—can you believe it!—who make seamstresses come

---

[29] *CF* 138.
[30] *CF* 68.

from Le Mans to sew their dresses for fear that the dressmakers in Alençon would reveal what their dresses look like before the celebration takes place. Isn't that ludicrous?"[31]

Her letters are sometimes in the style of Madame de Sévigné[32]: she enjoyed relating pithy anecdotes to amuse the family in Lisieux about all the scenes in Alençon that struck her. But she was always able to recognize her own faults: "I had the cowardice to mock Mrs. Y. I have infinite regret about that. I don't know why I have no sympathy for her since she's been nothing but good and helpful to me. I, who detest ingrates, can only detest myself now since I am nothing but a real ingrate myself. I want to convert in earnest and I've begun to do that, since for some time now I take every opportunity to say nice things about this lady. That's much more easily done since she is an excellent person who is worth more than all those who mock her, starting with me!"[33]

Louis and Zélie weren't turned in on themselves but instead were attentive to what was happening around them. They read La Croix[34] regularly, staying informed about local and national political developments because the anticlericalism of the time placed Catholics in jeopardy. Zélie was shocked to learn about the assassination of the archbishop of Paris and sixty-four priests during the time of the Commune. Listening to the prognosticators of ill omen, she feared for several months there would be a revolution. But her good sense won out: "The troubles have not come as predicted. I do not expect any will come for this year, and I have firmly decided not to listen to any prophet or predic-

---

[31] *CF* 54.

[32] A seventeenth-century French writer famous for her witty letters to her daughter.

[33] *CF* 75.

[34] A general-interest Catholic newspaper in France whose name means "The Cross."

tion. I'm starting to become a very skeptical person."[35] After this experience, like other women in her time, she left politics to her husband. "I pay no more attention to external events than my little Thérèse does,"[36] she wrote in 1874 when Thérèse was one year old.

Louis discussed politics with his friends and his brother-in-law and later even tried to introduce his views on the subject to Thérèse. Thérèse concluded, although we can doubt her objectivity, that if her father had been the king of France, things would have gone the best way possible in the best of all worlds. Meanwhile, Louis didn't get involved in politics. His fight was on another level. He preferred concrete assistance to the poor around him rather than the grand declarations of leaders, and he preferred prayer rather than demonstrations. This is one reason that after the war in 1870 he joined 20,000 participants in an enormous pilgrimage to Chartres to pray for the nation. He had to sleep in an underground chapel where Masses were being said all night. He went back there again in 1873 and wrote to Pauline, "Pray hard, little one, for the success of the pilgrimage to Chartres that I want to be part of; it will bring numerous pilgrims in our beautiful France to the feet of the Blessed Virgin so that we may obtain the graces that our country needs so much in order to be worthy of its past."[37] There is no doubt that he would have resonated with St. John Paul II's famous question, "France, eldest daughter of the Church, what have you done with your baptism?"[38]

Louis and Zélie were Catholics of their time for whom faith and patriotism were intertwined, living in fear of the anticlerical left and at the same time holding a firm conviction that the

---

[35] *CF* 80.

[36] *CF* 120.

[37] *CF* 102-a.

[38] Pope John Paul II, on his first pastoral visit to France as pope in 1980.

Lord was sustaining their country. The anticlericalism was a reality, though we have only a dim idea of it today. Louis, when he returned from a pilgrimage to Lourdes in 1873, was mocked in the train station in Lisieux because he was wearing a little red cross, and he was almost taken to the police station under the pretext that the mayor had forbidden pilgrims from coming back in procession. The disputes between Catholics and anticlerical groups increased during their lives, but in dealing with them the Martins always affirmed their faith in a nonviolent way.

Chapter 3

GOD FIRST

A reader might be surprised at focusing on the Martins' faith before looking at their family life and work. In so doing, however, we're following in the "spirit" of the Martins which can be summarized in two words: "God first."[39] It's impossible to understand the other aspects of their lives without reference to the source that guided them in all things.

The goal of Louis and Zélie, the dream of their youth and what they pursued all their lives, was holiness. "I want to be a saint,"[40] Zélie affirmed, while Louis confided to his daughters, "Yes, I have a goal, and it is to love God with all my heart."[41] What did people mean by holiness at that time? The best way to achieve it was to be consecrated, or do miracles, or die a martyr, or even all three together. It would take the coming of the Martins' daughter and the Second Vatican Council to remind us that holiness is accessible to everyone and required of everyone. This is still not completely clear in people's minds today.

Louis and Zélie demonstrate that holiness is possible through the simple life of spouses. If in the fervor of youth they

---

[39] This was Joan of Arc's motto that Louis, in turn, took up.

[40] *CF* 110.

[41] *LT*, see Letter by Sister Marie of the Sacred Heart (Marie) to Sister Agnes of Jesus (Pauline), May 21, 1889.

initially turned to the ideal represented by the consecrated life, they learned little by little from the Lord that holiness doesn't reside in one's state in life but in a trusting and loving response to God's call in daily life. In ordinary life, where joys and crosses alternate, they gave themselves fully to God and to their neighbor, abandoning themselves to his will in all things. They achieved a holiness that was far from the more or less spectacular examples that were being presented in the hagiography of their day. Theirs was a holiness anchored in the real and the ordinary, which the Church is highlighting today.

The Martins' desire for holiness wasn't capricious. They took all the means available to reach it, especially all the preferred means of sanctification accessible to all Catholics: the sacraments, prayer, and parish life.

The Eucharist was, first of all, the center of their lives and the first activity of each day. At that time receiving the Eucharist at Mass was not a given. To receive Communion in the state of grace certainly implied regular confession and faithfulness to God's commandments, but a concern to receive Christ appropriately was taken to extremes back then and deprived people of the grace of daily Communion. Having great hunger for the Eucharist, Louis and Zélie took Communion as often as possible: one or more times a week and all the First Fridays of the month. In being the first to arrive at morning Mass at 5:30 a.m., Louis and Zélie functioned, without their knowing it, like a pre-alarm clock. When the neighbors heard the first door on the street being closed, they would say, "It's that Martin couple going to church, so we still have time to sleep." Participating at Mass was less of an obligation for them than a privileged time in their Christian life.

Communion, above all, brought them joy, and that predilection was something they passed on to their children from their earliest years. "For a few weeks now we had taken her [little

Thérèse] out on Sunday. She had not gone to *Matthe*, as she called it. In coming home from our walk, she let out piercing screams saying that she wanted to go to *Matthe*. She opened the door and took off under torrential rain in the direction of the church. We ran after her to bring her back home, and her crying lasted a good hour. . . . She said to me loudly in church, "I just went to *Matthe*! I *prayded* to God."[42]

Participation at Mass wasn't just a routine for them but a vital necessity, a refreshment and feast, even though they experienced the well-known difficulties that fatigue and worry can bring: "This morning I was sleeping as I dressed myself; I was almost sleeping as I was walking; I was sleeping at the first Mass when I was on my knees, standing up, sitting down, and as I prayed."[43] On another occasion, Zélie said, "There was sermon, but I am not sure what was preached because I was so absorbed in my thoughts."[44] Distraction and drowsiness were also Zélie's lot, but meanwhile grace was working during Masses that she experienced without ecstasy: "This morning during Mass I had such dark thoughts about this [fear of losing the baby] that I was completely distressed"; however, demonstrating the fruit of this Mass, she added, "The best thing to do is to put everything back in God's hands and calmly wait for events to unfold in abandonment to his will."[45]

The Martins' holiness in relationship to the Eucharist was evident in the importance they accorded it, not in any visible fervor. We see its importance for them first in the intense preparation that preceded every Communion for themselves and for the children as well. They didn't hesitate to separate themselves

---

[42] *CF* 130.
[43] *CF* 156.
[44] *CF* 128.
[45] *CF* 45.

from their daughter Léonie by sending her to boarding school at the Visitation Monastery with the single goal of having her prepare well for her first Communion. Preparing to receive God requires using all the small means in daily life—"It is a constant preparation that goes on every day," according to Zélie[46]—as well as using more significant measures: "I took her [Léonie] last Tuesday on pilgrimage to the Immaculate Conception at Séez so that she could obtain the grace to make a good First Communion."[47] Zélie knew that receiving this preparation was a grace in itself, and she blessed God when she saw Léonie prepare fervently. This preparation was unconnected to the action of grace that follows the receiving of every Eucharist, however: "I attended three Masses this morning. I went to the one at 6:00, I did my thanksgivings and said my prayers during the one at 7:00, and then I went back for the High Mass."[48]

Mass was a priority, so all other activities were organized around it. It could require different arrangements, and we can admire the careful manner in which Zélie made provisions for it: "When you come home, dear Pauline, it will be more difficult; you like to sleep in the morning and to go to bed late. . . . I will figure out a way for both of you [Marie and Pauline] to go [to Mass] at different times. If at that time I am not still making Alençon lace, it will be very simple, but if not, I will have a dilemma. Well, we will just figure something out."[49] Both Louis and Zélie maintained faithfulness to the Eucharist to a heroic degree when, in their final illnesses, they devoted their minimal capacity for movement to receiving it despite their suffering. They didn't go to Mass as "consumers" but rather with the immense respect

---

[46] *CF* 200.
[47] *CF* 125.
[48] *CF* 108.
[49] *CF* 172.

of those who know and love the ineffable mystery, the mystery of a God who abased himself to give himself to us.

Recognizing the Eucharist as the most powerful prayer, they never ceased having recourse to it on behalf of the living as much as on behalf of the dead. Zélie, with a touch of humor, attributed the success of her brother's exams to the Mass she offered for that intention. The Martins preferred to offer Masses for the dead instead of flower bouquets, and they placed every important intention on the Eucharistic table. With a group of friends in Alençon, Louis also participated every month in Nocturnal Eucharistic Adoration; it was so meaningful for him that he organized the Nocturnal Adoration in Lisieux.

The Martins had great respect for every sacrament, in addition to the Eucharist. They preferred that an infant receive baptism almost immediately. They believed from the bottom of their hearts that baptism, by which a newborn passes through the death and resurrection of Christ, brings salvation to that soul, and that had more value in their eyes than the newborn's life. God always came first. And they delighted in distributing more than four pounds of fine candies to all the children present, adding to the joy of the baptism.

They each had a regular confessor and considered the Sacrament of Reconciliation the privileged instrument of divine mercy, not a burden.

The Martins were bonded to their parish. The Catholic environment of Alençon together with the anticlerical political context resulted in the vivid intermingling of national and spiritual interests. In general, the liveliness of the Christian faith at that time was all on the surface, an outward rather than an inward reality. The Martins, however, while affirming their faith, didn't engage in polemics and simply participated in the planned parish activities. They took part in liturgical feasts, processions, retreats, and the missions that took place no matter who the more-or-less appreciated preacher was: "For eight days now, we have had two missionaries who are giving three sermons a day. Neither one preaches better than the other, in my opinion. We go hear them anyway out of duty, and for me at least, it is an extra penance."[50] Zélie still had a critical spirit, but she made the best of everything.

Sunday the whole household went to High Mass, vespers, and sometimes the Divine Office evening prayers. Louis and Zélie appreciated beautiful liturgies. Zélie was disappointed about a particular ceremony in the month of May, commenting: "We hear unbearable songs that are like cooing that no one can understand; one would think we were at a café-concert and that annoys me! In earlier times, singing was more pious, so it seems that we are being more progressive now!"[51]—a reflection familiar to many people today!

Louis and Zélie were members of multiple pious associations and enrolled their children in them too. These associations and brotherhoods gathered for small monthly meetings to pray for certain intentions. Zélie said she wasn't always faithful to these obligations but never stopped trying to be faithful. She also visited the nearby convent of Poor Clare sisters for advice and prayer. As a Third Order Franciscan, she was quite attuned to the spirituality of *il Poverello* (St. Francis of Assisi), whose joyful freedom helped her to detach from whatever rigidity in the faith she had received from her parents, and she participated in meetings for the members of the Third Order. She cheerfully said that the simple view of a Capuchin converted her, so she didn't hesitate, even with a fever and a work overload, to get up at dawn for two weeks to attend a mission preached by one of them. In his own way Louis shared the friendship his wife

---

[50] *CF* 130.
[51] *CF* 159.

had for the Franciscan family by bringing all his fishing catch to the Poor Clares.

For the Martins, prayer didn't stop at the church door. Their silent and solitary professional work was favorable for recollection, and times of prayer regulated the rhythm of the day: Mass in the morning, Benediction, and grace at each meal, and at night the whole family joined together in prayer. Once the children were in bed and the last tasks of the day were finished, Louis and Zélie spent one last time before the Lord before going to bed.

For the special intentions confided to her, Zélie liked to do a novena to the Sacred Heart, St. Joseph, or other saints, depending on the circumstances. Knowing the power of united prayer to move God's heart, she often asked another member of the family to join her. The couple honored the Rosary and Zélie confided one day to her friend Philomène Tessier that she would like to be a simple little woman saying her Rosary at the back of the church and be unknown to everyone. Between her work and her children, Zélie lacked time to pray, which was distressing for someone who had such a hunger for God. As for Louis, he preferred the prayer of pilgrimage for obtaining graces as well as for thanking the Lord. Prayer would take on a greater and greater place in his life, as it did for his wife.

The role of asceticism emerges clearly in their life of prayer and their presence before God. When a soul is placed under God's light, it discovers the requirements of pure divinity, according to the Carmelite priest Father Marie-Eugène.[52] The Martins' asceticism took on forms that came to them from liturgical life and from the events of the day. In addition, they scrupulously observed all the fasts prescribed by the Church but added some-

---

[52] See Father Marie-Eugene de L'Enfant Jésus, O.C.D., *Je veux voir Dieu* [*I Want to See God*] (Venasque: Editions du Carmel, 1957), 80.

thing absolute of their own: they would eat nothing until noon and at night they ate only a light meal—except, of course, when Zélie was pregnant. If a person invited himself or herself unexpectedly, a nice dinner was served that had to be eaten alone! Fasting was not any easier for them than for other people. Zélie admitted that directly: "We are doing full-time penitence. Fortunately it will soon be over, because I am suffering from this fasting and abstinence! It is not, though, a very difficult mortification, but I am weary for my stomach's sake, and above all I am so lax that I would not be doing this at all if I listened to my nature."[53]

Today the word asceticism seems out of date. The *Catechism of the Catholic Church*, however, speaks of its benefits: "The way of perfection passes by way of the Cross. There is no holiness without renunciation and spiritual battle. Spiritual progress entails the ascetics and mortification that gradually lead to living in the peace and joy of the Beatitudes."[54] It was in this spirit that Louis practiced a quite discreet but firm asceticism: he forbade himself from smoking, crossing his legs, drinking between meals, and drawing closer to the fire unless necessary. He traveled in third class and ate poor quality bread that was generally meant for the poor. These were minor sacrifices that were not ends in themselves but that gave him a detachment from material things. He told his daughter Marie, who wondered about these austerities, that it was because he took Communion often. That was the Martin logic: God always came first. They pursued this life with God throughout the day. Far from being harmful to their work, their time with the children, and their social life, it enriched all their activities. One need not look elsewhere to explain the source of their love for one another, for their daughters, for their neigh-

---

[53] *CF* 130.
[54] *CCC* 2015.

bors, and even for the quality of their work. They could have had as their motto, "Our hearts with God above, our feet on the ground."

Martin spirituality can be defined by three principles: the sovereignty of God, confidence in his Providence, and abandonment to his will.

God was indeed first in their hearts and their lives. Louis and Zélie were deeply conscious of his grandeur and love, keeping in mind that God is our origin, the only true reality, and our goal. There is a text from Félicité Robert Lammenais that Zélie knew by heart and that she often recited to her daughters: "Oh! Speak to me of the mysteries of this world that my desires foreshadow, into which my soul, weary of the shadows of the earth, aspires to immerse itself. Speak to me of the One who made it and fills it with himself and who alone can fill the immense void that he created in me."[55] Both of them in their own way were living out Augustine's famous saying that we are made for God, and our hearts will not rest until they rest in him. Even when they took pleasure in something here below, Louis and Zélie located the fullness of happiness only in heaven, so their gaze was constantly turned upward. Thérèse would later confirm that herself: "Heaven is the place toward which all their actions and desires tended."[56]

In Zélie's letters we discover the impact of this hope in their lives. At the beginning of their marriage, she lived a life of great happiness and wrote about it to her brother, telling him that the Blessed Mother "will help you to succeed in this world and

---

[55] Hugues Félicité Robert de Lammenais, a nineteenth-century Catholic priest and philosopher. The quote is from *Amschaspands et Darvands* (Brussells: Meline, Cans et Cie, 1843), p. 295.

[56] *LT* 266, Letter from Thérèse to Father Adolphe Roulland, May 9, 1897.

then give you an eternity of happiness."[57] Zélie was not one to champion a disincarnated spirituality that rejects every kind of earthly joy. Like every human being she wanted happiness. But at the end of her life, worn down by sorrows, worries, and illness, she wrote, "[The Blessed Virgin] has told all of us, as she did Bernadette, 'I will make you happy, not in this world but in the next.'"[58] Zélie experienced the weight of the cross in her life and—contrary to those who sell canned happiness—she didn't believe that happiness in this world was truly possible. She freely philosophized, "True happiness is not in this world, and we are wasting time to look for it here."[59] This was a constant theme in her letters.

Is that pessimism? Or is it realism from someone who ascribes such a high value to the idea of happiness that she cannot find it in things that fade away? In the three preceding quotations from her, one element is constant: the hope of happiness in heaven. If it is not to be found here below, it is because "God in his wisdom wanted it that way to make us remember that the earth is not our true home."[60] Thérèse later said the same thing. Like their daughter, the Martin spouses remind our materialistic world that our destiny isn't here below and people must not be mistaken about what they seek. Look for happiness, yes, but in heaven, where it truly is to be found. Thérèse would explicitly clarify that heaven is not a strange or future reality, but the life of God himself who already dwells in us.

The God of the Martins was not, despite all this, a distant God. As Zélie testified personally, "When I think of what God, in

---

[57] *CF* 1.
[58] *CF* 210.
[59] *CF* 31.
[60] *CF* 7.

whom I have placed all my confidence and in whose hands I have entrusted all my affairs, has done for me and my husband, I cannot doubt that his divine Providence watches over his children with special care."[61] On another occasion she said, "I know God is taking care of me."[62] For the Martins, God is a "good Father" who was actually part of the family. They relied on him and knew that nothing bad could happen to them under his protection, even in the midst of the most sorrowful trials. "The one who hopes in God will never be put to shame" became a family saying, as well as the saying that "God only gives us what we can bear." (This particular language of their day has since been adjusted: God does not "give" us trials but permits them.)

And the Martins knew that God, far from being an angry and vengeful offended party, was, on the contrary, a God who watched over them with love. They acknowledged his hand in the great graces of their lives: their marriage, their children, their success in their work, but also their decisions. When a serious choice proved to be providentially judicious, they thanked God, persuaded that he had been inspiring and guiding them. God was too close not to be interested in them.

He would not let them fall . . . even literally, as Zélie experienced. One day when she was leaving for Mass, she put baby Thérèse in her own bed, which she often did, but forgot to wedge the crib against the edge of the bed to keep the baby from rolling off. How surprised she was that day when, returning home, she found the baby quietly sitting on a chair facing the bed that, according to all indications, would not have been possible. "I could not understand how she fell in such a way as to be sitting on that chair since she had been in bed. I thank God that nothing happened to her. It was really providential; she should have rolled

---

[61] *CF* 1.
[62] *CF* 156.

down onto the floor. Her good angel was watching over her, and the souls in purgatory to whom I pray every day for the little one protected her. That's the only way I can explain it. . . . You can think what you want about it!"[63] In these small events of life, Louis and Zélie recognized the goodness of God and thanked him. Providence was a reality they experienced and on which they relied.

Their abandonment to his will flowed from this confidence in the goodness of God and his care. Louis and Zélie progressively put their whole lives in his hands and let him guide them. This attitude isn't innate: no one is born a saint, one has to become a saint. Zélie herself commented on this evolution: "I didn't forget December 8, 1860," she wrote sixteen years later. "This was the day that I prayed to our Heavenly Mother to give me a little Pauline. But I cannot think of it without laughing because I was just like a child who demands a doll from her mother, and I went about it the same way. I wanted a Pauline just like the one I have, and I dotted my 'i's in fear that the Blessed Mother would not understand exactly what I wanted."[64] In 1860 it was still *her* will that she was asking God to fulfill, speaking to him as a sort of distributor of grace who was too far away to really understand her.

With the passing of years and the events of her life, she became more and more aware that God, who knew her better than she knew herself, understood her needs without her having to detail them and "dot all her 'i's." She increasingly experienced his goodness. This dynamic woman, who was quite capable of leading her own life, began to seek her own will less and less, abandoning herself to the will of her "good" God. From a prayer

---

[63] *CF* 119.
[64] *CF* 147.

that was a naive and somewhat egocentric demand, Zélie moved to Mary's *Fiat*. She no longer presented herself to God as a demanding and anxious child—"I want this, I want that"—but as a humble, confident little child who knows she can count on the goodness of her Father: "Let it be to me according to your word" (Lk 1:38). This is the same attitude that Thérèse would express and that she first experienced through the example of her parents.

Louis and Zélie didn't cease surrendering their wills to God's will and wanted his will to be manifested in events and in their relatives' decisions. To surrender one's will is not fashionable, and our society has confused it with the loss of liberty. The example of the Martins is enlightening. They teach us that the greatest liberty is not in the arbitrary exercise of our own egotistical will and desires but in submitting—as paradoxical as it may seem—to the will of our Father. Set free from the slavery that sin represents, the Martins were free to love and didn't deprive themselves of love. The surrender of our wills means that we recognize we are not all-powerful and that we don't control events. The Martins surrendered so well that in the face of the great sufferings in their lives, as we shall see again and again, they continued to say, *Fiat*. Accepting to live the experience of suffering doesn't mean accepting suffering; it means accepting to go from the reality of suffering to living it out in love. Zélie wrote, "When it is a question of a real misfortune, I am completely resigned and I wait for help from God with confidence."[65]

Dr. Robert Cadéot's study of the recurring use of the word "resignation" by the Martins is enlightening. The word can be confusing today because its meaning has changed in one century.

---

[65] *CF* 140.

Zélie accepts the reality of suffering in union with the cross of Christ. To express that, she uses the word "resignation" that was much in use in the nineteenth century. But semantics can play tricks on us. In the dictionary we can find synonyms like "abdication, submission, apathy, relinquishment, fatalism." For Zélie that word does not evoke the inertia of the quietists or the sorrow of those who believe in sorrow for sorrow's sake, and still less does it mean apathy, relinquishment, and fatalism. For her, as for her daughter Thérèse who will later also occasionally use that word, "resignation" is a voluntary abandonment of one's will to the love of God through which she accepts experiencing her sufferings in the hope of heaven.[66]

Abandonment to God's will and resignation in the midst of trials were not merely passive attitudes with the Martins. At the heart of their spirituality was an attitude of offering. All their suffering was offered to the Lord, in a manner Pope Benedict XVI explains in his encyclical *Spe Salvi* (*Saved in Hope*):

> There used to be a form of devotion—perhaps less practiced today but quite widespread not long ago—that included the idea of "offering up" the minor daily hardships that continually strike at us like irritating "jabs," thereby giving them a meaning. . . . What does it mean to offer something up? Those who did so were convinced that they could insert these little annoyances into Christ's great "com-passion" so that they somehow became part of the treasury of compassion so greatly needed by the human race. In this way, even the small inconveniences

---

[66] Robert Cadéot, *Zélie Martin, mère incomparable de St. Thérèse de l'Enfant Jésus* (Paris: Fr.-X de Guibert, 1996), p. 103.

of daily life could acquire meaning and contribute to the economy of good and of human love. Maybe we should consider whether it might be judicious to revive this practice ourselves.[67]

In developing the habit of offering up the small vexations of the day—in particular for the salvation of souls—the Martin spouses became capable of offering up their greater trials and also of offering up themselves. The Martins' spirituality involved a self-sacrificing spirituality lived to the fullest, and they transmitted that approach to their children. Thérèse is a perfect example of that.

A chapter on the spirituality of the Martins can't conclude without recalling the place that Mary had in their hearts. They had a devotional, filial love for her, praying to her every day and celebrating her in all possible ways. Both of them wore a scapular, the only piece of clothing that was found intact upon their exhumation. They had each of their children wear one too, because they wanted them protected under the mantle of the Blessed Virgin. The Martins gathered together every evening around the statue of the Virgin to pray. That statue, known as Our Lady of the Smile, can be found today at Thérèse's shrine in Lisieux. A three-foot-high reproduction shows Our Lady without a veil and with her hands open to receive children and to distribute graces. Louis and Zélie loved this Virgin in particular—the statue's fingers had to be replaced because of being kissed so often. Their daughter Marie, thinking that the statue was too big, had proposed replacing it, but Zélie cried out that as long as she lived, that Blessed Virgin would not leave their house. At the beginning of the month of May, Mary's month, they decorated the

---

[67] Benedict XVI, *Spe Salvi* (*Saved in Hope*), n. 40, November 30, 2007.

statue in a special way. Louis wanted it to have garlands of flower petals. Marie, when she was in charge of decorating it one day, expressed her annoyance: "Maman is too difficult, more difficult than the Blessed Virgin! We need to have white hawthorn that goes up to the ceiling, walls covered with greenery, etc. etc."[68] Nothing was too beautiful for a Mother who was so well loved.

My purpose in recounting the above is not to make a comparative study of the Martins' spirituality and that of their daughter, but to draw attention to Thérèse's spiritual heritage. The major orientations of her "little way" were none other than those of her parents' spirituality applied in her own way. The education of the Martin daughters, as we will see, was entirely shaped by the spirituality of their parents.

---

[68] *LT*, Letter from Marie Martin to Pauline, May 9, 1877.

Chapter 4

THE VOCATION OF PARENTS

The education of their children was as much a vocation as a joy for the Martin couple. Zélie exclaimed, "I am crazy about children; I was born to give birth to them."[69] Louis felt the same way, and from the beginning they wanted to have many. "We have five already," Zélie wrote in 1868, "without counting those that might arrive, because I hope to have three or four more!"[70] Each pregnancy was a joy, each new child a gift from heaven. They knew the delight and pride of all parents: "You don't know how good and affectionate she is," Zélie wrote about Pauline. "She hugs us all the time without our asking; she blows kisses to 'good Jesus'; she doesn't speak but she understands everything; she's a unique child."[71] Zélie's letters are full of a mother's happiness that never left her: "If you had seen the two oldest ones today and how nice they looked, everybody was admiring them and couldn't take their eyes off of them. And I was beaming and said to myself, 'They are mine!'"[72]

Zélie was an entirely happy mother. The family letters are studded with scenes of family joy: "I was glad to see my little Joseph on the first of the year [after being away with his wet

---

[69] *CF* 83.
[70] *CF* 32.
[71] *CF* 1.
[72] *CF* 13.

nurse]. For his New Year's gift, I dressed him like a prince. If you only knew how handsome he is and how heartily he laughed! My husband said, 'You're parading him around like the wooden statue of a saint.'"[73] They were equally well acquainted with the difficulties of young parents, however: enduring a baby crying for "thirty-six hours without stopping,"[74] the squabbles between sisters, the nights of two hours of sleep. But they considered it a small price to pay. According to Zélie, "It's such a sweet task to take care of small children!"[75]

A sweet task, but one for which the Martins spared themselves no pain, having their children on all occasions come before themselves. "If you had as many [children] as I do," Zélie wrote to the Guérin family, "it would require much self-denial and the desire to enrich heaven with new members of the chosen."[76] After the birth of the first Thérèse, Zélie recounted how she got up at 6:00 a.m. to help the woman she had hired to take care of her (!) and then took care of the other children herself before going back to work on her orders for lace. She ended by saying, "Tell me again that I am not strong!"[77]

Despite all her work, she took time to play with the children: "I had fun . . . but I had to fill an order for lace that was urgent, so I had to make up for lost time by staying up until 1:00 in the morning."[78] She willingly sacrificed her minimal leisure time when she took the older children to the Exposition in Alençon, admitting that she found it utterly boring. Louis was no less active than his wife in these matters: "The sacrifices he makes for

---

[73] *CF* 21.
[74] *CF* 23.
[75] *CF* 31.
[76] *CF* 50.
[77] *CF* 59.
[78] *CF* 21.

her [Thérèse] day and night are unbelievable."[79] Louis and Zélie gave themselves without counting the cost: "We were living only for them now."[80]

They were able to educate only six of their nine children since death removed three too early from their affection. Their first child was Marie, who revealed to them their joyful vocation as parents. She was born on February 22, 1860. Early on she manifested a nonconformist spirit, which Father Piat admirably described: "Independent and fervent about her liberty, but with an exquisite sensitivity, disliking any complexity, forthright and frank, with original witticisms and at times manifestations of a shyness that made her seem rude and enigmatic." [81]

On September 7, 1861, Pauline entered the family and was an equally engaging child: "With a vivacity that called for restraint, she was sympathetic and lively like her mother, with a similar harmonious combination of solid and brilliant qualities that suit an individual for the exercise of authority."[82] These two little ones soon became inseparable. By temperament, Louis felt closer to Marie while Zélie's letters show her to have had a special affection for Pauline. The Martins didn't succeed in hiding this preference from their children, and that could have at times been a source of suffering for the other children, even for these two. During her adolescence Pauline had to take on the role of being her mother's confidant, which couldn't have been easy.

But Louis and Zélie had enough love to go around for all their children, not just the older ones. This is evident in all their efforts for their third daughter, Léonie, who was born on June 3, 1863. Unlike her first two sisters, she was difficult from birth,

---

[79] *CF* 173.
[80] *CF* 192.
[81] *HF* 142.
[82] Ibid.

as much because of her health as her character, but that never discouraged the parents from persevering on the child's behalf.

On October 13, 1864, Hélène made her appearance, a lovely child whose great beauty was the pride of Louis and Zélie. The three children who came next (Joseph-Louis, Joseph-Jean-Baptiste, and Mélanie-Thérèse) never reached the age of one, so it was with a mixture of joy and worry that they welcomed Céline on April 28, 1869. Céline's health was fragile, but she was a sensitive, intelligent child who could not easily be separated from her baby sister Thérèse, who was born on January 2, 1873.

There's a story behind the choice of Thérèse's name. In the Martin family, whether the baby was a girl or a boy, everyone's first name was Marie because Louis and Zélie wanted the patronage of the Blessed Virgin for all their children. But after this given, things could get complicated. During one pregnancy Zélie felt that the baby was strong and speculated it was a boy. Since the Martins loved St. Joseph almost as much as Mary, Zélie naturally thought, for the third time, of giving that name to the baby who was about to be born. But her sister in Le Mans didn't like that name because she wanted to have her patron saint's name in the family. Zélie recounted, "Before the baby was born, she [Zélie's sister] had written me, believing it would be a boy, and had said I should name him Francis and not Joseph, as if she suspected that good St. Joseph had taken away the other babies!"[83] Zélie immediately replied that whether the baby died because of it or lived because of it, "I would call him Joseph."[84]

Once the "he" turned into a "she" at birth, however, Zélie made a few concessions and accepted calling the baby girl Marie Françoise Thérèse with the stipulation that "Thérèse" would be the name used by the family. But when Thérèse subsequently

---

[83] *CF* 87.
[84] Ibid.

became sick as well, and they informed the sister of Le Mans of that, she zealously prayed to St. Francis de Sales with extraordinary fervor and vowed that if the little baby were healed, she should be called Françoise by the family! The baby got better (well before the vow was made, apparently), but Zélie, with her habitual good common sense, took offense at Sister Marie-Dosithée's position: "What does it matter to St. Francis de Sales whether the baby is called one name or the other? My refusal on this issue could not be a reason to make her die!"[85] Thérèse would be called Thérèse, and Zélie concluded: "I would not want to hurt my sister because she is so good, and she loves us so much! But this time she astonishes me."[86]

Louis and Zélie took charge of other members of the family. Until they moved in 1871, they lived with their parents. Mr. and Mrs. Martin lived on the top floor of the house, and there Pierre-François Martin died in 1865. In 1867, Zélie had her father, who was now widowed and had trouble taking care of himself, come live with them. But she had to resort to a ruse to persuade him: "When I talked to him about his coming here he was very angry, but I told him I could not get by without him and he was such a help to me, so I entreated him to stay. My husband joined me in that request, so he shuffled off and said nothing, and I convinced him."[87] Zélie took care of the elderly man devotedly until his death in 1868, with the assistance of Louis who would not have done less for his own father. His wife, moved by this, testified, "You could not meet one in a hundred who is as good as he is to his father-in-law."[88]

---

85 Ibid.
86 Ibid.
87 *CF* 17.
88 *CF* 20.

There was also a domestic servant who lived on the premises. To be a maid at the Martins was the equivalent of being a nanny or a chief housekeeper and being part of the family. Zélie affirmed, "I don't treat the servants less well than my children."[89] She never gave them leftovers to eat, preferring to eat those herself. Everyone told her, to no avail, that she didn't know how to let herself be served, but she maintained a stance about servants that was quite original for that era: "They need to feel that we love them; we need to show them friendliness and not be too formal with them."[90] There was no hypocrisy in that because she really loved her maid, Louise Marais, who worked for the family for eleven years. Zélie served her as much as she was served by her. So, in 1871, when they were in the process of moving to Rue Saint-Blaise and Louise fell gravely ill, Zélie nursed her day and night for three weeks. Another time, Zélie, who was sick herself, spent part of her nights taking care of her maid. "I am really fond of her, as she is of me."[91] Even though Louise was always ill and needed a lot of help to do her work, Zélie never dreamed of letting her go.

With all those little girls around, the atmosphere in the Martin house wasn't sad. Louis and Zélie, despite their trials, made sure that cheerfulness reigned in the home. The joys were simple: little games, songs, and above all the joy of being together. The girls frequently interrupted Zélie in her correspondence as they ran from one end of the house to the other smiling and dancing for joy. In the Martin family charity ruled—they often told one another of their love, one for the other. Zélie wrote to Pauline, for example, "So, you see, my affection for you grows day by day;

---

[89] *CF* 29.
[90] Ibid.
[91] *CF* 68.

you are my joy and happiness."[92] Each tried to please the others with small gifts, acts of service, or undivided attention. Zélie gave her girls what she herself had not received: a love full of tenderness and a happy, warm atmosphere. Louis himself had a real gift for taking care of children. He put himself on their level, told them stories and played with them, singing to them in his beautiful voice from his immense repertoire of old French songs, and imitating a thousand sounds of nature or the Norman dialect for his amazed and joyful daughters.

He wasn't reluctant to add firmness to his customary gentleness and tenderness. Louis would rather become angry than let his darling little ones do things out of frivolous impulse. The girls had to finish their plates at mealtimes no matter what. When the pitch would rise among the girls, he only had to say, "Peace, children." Zélie similarly applied a strict method with Pauline: "I have to tell you that I didn't spoil her. Even though she was still so young, I didn't let her get away with anything, but without making a martyr out of her, and she had to give in."[93] The mother sensed, in fact, that this child had a strong character and a liveliness that could become unbearable and prideful if not appropriately channeled.

This method wasn't used with all the children. Louis and Zélie didn't apply a single ideal model of education across the board, but used clear discernment to give each child what she needed. They were all well treated, however, which they unanimously testified to during the beatification process for Thérèse. Declaring they were not spoiled, they described their mother as watching over the souls of her children with great care, never leaving the smallest fault unchecked. It was a good, effective education, done attentively and carefully.

---

[92] *CF* 141.
[93] *CF* 44.

The Martin parents had a sense of authority, but they never abused it: "Brutality never converted anybody; it only makes people slaves," Zélie wrote about Léonie,[94] and during that era such an assertion was quite bold. Louis and Zélie established a climate of trust, and Céline later said that the daughters obeyed out of love. "Trust was the heart of this education," Father Piat said. "Having suffered in her youth from a regime of cold, coerced restraint inflicted by her mother, Mrs. Martin resolved at all costs to spare her children from such an experience. She wanted them to be open, expansive, and fully blossomed. Léonie's withdrawn nature at certain periods disconcerted and troubled her. She knew the temptations of a soul tightly closed in on itself and the danger of inner repression. Her letters show her to be diligent and clear about knowing the members of her household and how to treat each of them."[95]

The younger ones were a bit spoiled, but with prudence: "The older children have enough toys now for the rest of their youth. They take care of their things because I do not give them things to misuse."[96] Every Christmas the girls received presents from their parents, and at New Year's there was always a big feast. They would receive a box full of things from the Guérin family who were very generous, much to Zélie's consternation. Seeing such marvelous gifts the youngest ones were silent with surprise while the older ones pranced around hard enough to "wear out the floor!"[97]

Every year the same scenes of family fun would occur: "When their father unpacked the toys, I wish you could have seen Thérèse especially! We had told her, 'There are nice toys

---

[94] *CF* 195.

[95] *HF*, p. 138.

[96] *CF* 21.

[97] *CF* 149. This is said in reference particularly to Céline.

in there that your aunt in Lisieux sent.' She clapped her hands. When I was pressing on top of the trunk to help my husband open it, she kept crying out in anguish, 'Maman, you are going to break my nice toys!' She was pulling on my dress to make me stop. But when she saw her pretty little doll house, she was dumbstruck for a moment. She is a child who has a deep reaction to things."[98]

The Martin children had dolls, dish sets for dolls, books (they appreciated, among others, the Countess of Ségur[99]), and numerous other toys that their father liked to make for them himself. The parents, however, refused to buy them anything superfluous, even when Marie and Pauline would present the eternal argument, "But all our friends have one!"

Although Zélie was not the least bit taken with fashion, she liked to dress her children well, making clothes for them that made them "as pretty as little loves"[100] according to her. Her guideline in the matter was to have them "dressed well while remaining simple,"[101] and she admitted making some concessions to fashion for her children when they were in good taste. She wrote a very modern paragraph on slavery to fashion in a letter to her sister-in-law.

Taking walks was the great pastime for the Martin girls: accompanying Papa as he went fishing, walking through the surrounding countryside, or best of all spending the afternoon on Louis's small property, the Pavilion, having fun and cultivating the small section of the garden designated to each child. "Yesterday morning, Céline was pestering your father to bring her and

---

[98] *CF* 126.

[99] A nineteenth-century French Catholic novelist of Russian birth, author of the 1858 novel *Les petites filles modèles* [*Little Model Girls*].

[100] *CF* 55. This is said in reference particularly to Céline.

[101] *CF* 146.

Thérèse to the Pavilion as he [had] done the day before. He said to her, 'Are you joking? Do you think I will take you there every day?' The little one was there playing with a wand and did not seem to be listening because she was so absorbed. While continuing her playing, she says to her sister, 'We cannot be so cheeky as to think that Papa would take us every day.' Your father laughed so hard."[102]

Every Sunday after vespers, the whole family went out, at times hiring a big open air carriage to go off and visit the region. One day two elderly women, knowing that the Martins planned such an excursion and that there was room in the carriage, asked to join the family. Zélie later said frankly that they were not very nice ladies. Marie's crying over the disappointment of not being together only as a family didn't help. The Martins welcomed the elderly ladies for the outing, giving their girls a lesson that none of them forgot: charity is practiced in good times and at inconvenient times, even when it upsets plans.[103]

In order to give their children the best possible formation, Louis and Zélie sent the two oldest ones to the Visitation Monastery in Le Mans where Sister Marie-Dosithée was. Zélie said of this arrangement that each time school reopened "you cannot imagine what it costs me to send them away from me, but we have to make sacrifices for their happiness."[104] Marie and Pauline felt the separation just as much, and no separation happens without tears. Zélie surprised herself one day—and God knows it was unusual—by weeping hot tears. They counted the days until vacation, which were rare at that time. That sacrifice, however, brought wonderful fruit. The two girls received a solid education

---

[102] *CF* 169.

[103] See *CF* 122 for the story.

[104] *CF* 55.

and spiritual formation at the Francis de Sales School that stood them in good stead all their lives. Marie could thus help form her younger sisters while Pauline acquired all the skills later needed to become a prioress at the Carmelite monastery in Lisieux. The life of the Visitation sisters, and in particular the life of their well-loved aunt there, inspired their religious vocations.

Sister Marie-Dosithée looked out for the schooling of her nieces, regularly sending reports to Alençon. Zélie, full of maternal pride, would subsequently tell her daughters in Lisieux about those good results. Marie and Pauline were more advanced than the other students their age, and Pauline was considered the best student in the whole school. Although the parents were proud of these honors, they didn't attach exaggerated importance to them. The following year Zélie couldn't even remember how many prizes Pauline had won. Of course, Louis and Zélie were happy and proud when their daughters brought home good results from school, but that wasn't what counted the most in their eyes. After they considered having Marie join a group called "the Children of the Blessed Virgin," which was a privilege accorded only to good students with exemplary behavior, Zélie insisted, "Above all, let her try to deserve such a beautiful title."[105]

It isn't difficult to link their academic success to the excellent education they received from their parents. The teachers were overjoyed with the behavior of Pauline and Marie, without telling the girls about it in order to protect their humility. More was always required of them so they could learn to give the best of themselves. The Martins chose the Visitation sisters not just because of Zélie's sister but especially because the spirit of firm gentleness that permeated the pedagogy of the Visitation sisters reflected their own pedagogy. Zélie described an example concerning some incidents with ink. At the school in Alençon,

---

[105] *CF* 110.

when Marie was six, she spilled ink and the teachers made her dip her hands in the ink and cover her face with it, something that years later still made her indignant. Pauline had the same accident at the Visitation Monastery, but the sisters, knowing she hadn't done it on purpose, cleaned up the ink and didn't scold her. A more profitable lesson. Zélie was particularly grateful, then, for the way the Visitation sisters dealt with Marie. Marie, so headstrong and unsociable, allowed herself to be softened by their gentleness.

Louis and Zélie's third daughter, Léonie, was their educational challenge. Since her birth she had piled up their worries about her health, and they noticed soon enough that this child was more difficult than the others. The reasons for her difficulties are more easily understood today. In addition to the suffering of her chronic illnesses, without doubt she was traumatized by the death of her sister Hélène. The Martin children, because of their ages, functioned as pairs: first Marie and Pauline, and later Céline and Thérèse. Léonie and Hélène should have been the pair in the middle. Born in 1863 and 1864, they were close in age, if not in character, and were play companions. Hélène died in 1870. It is precisely in the following weeks that Zélie's letters mention the first traces of Léonie's flawed character, now that she was left on her own.

Besides the shock of the death of someone so young, Léonie resented her new, uncomfortable position. She was too young to join the older ones but too old to be with the two youngest ones. She found herself isolated and turned inward. She frequently acted foolishly and impulsively, didn't keep her promises, lied, and she could become violently angry. Her difficulties only increased. When Léonie was nine, Zélie wrote: "I cannot analyze her character; however, even the most knowledgeable people would not be able to make heads or tails out of her. I hope in any case that a good seed will come forth from the earth one day. If I see that, I will sing my *Nunc dimittis*."[106]

That hope would be a saving factor for Léonie. Her parents never became discouraged, and Zélie never omitted commenting, alongside each account of the child's missteps and her own anxieties, that her daughter had a good heart deep down. Louis always called her "my good Léonie"[107] while her aunt in Le Mans went so far as to call her "the predestined one."[108] They looked at her with confidence, knowing her to be good and capable of getting out of her difficulties. Careful not to turn their child into the odd duck of the group, they created family solidarity around her, asking the other children to pray for her.

Counting on the success of her sister where she herself had failed, Zélie decided with Louis to send Léonie to the Visitation Monastery in January 1874. The little girl was eleven years old, but she looked like she was eight. Sister Marie-Dosithée took charge of her and, in the great tradition of St. Francis de Sales, made gentleness a priority: "The first month I scolded when she was not doing well, and it happened so often that it was all I was doing. . . . I could see that I was going to make the little one unhappy, which was not what I wanted; I wanted to be God's Providence for her. . . . I started to treat her with the greatest gentleness and avoided scolding her. I told her I saw she wanted to be good and please me, and I had faith in her. . . . That produced a magical result that was not just temporary but long-lasting, because it is a reasonable approach and I find her completely darling. . . . I will need to season sweetness with firmness again,

---

[106] *CF* 81. *Nunc dimittis* is the beginning of the prayer by Simeon in the Temple after he finally saw the awaited Messiah (see Lk 2:29-32).

[107] *CF* 225.

[108] *CF* 116. As a child, Léonie had been healed through the intercession of St. Margaret Mary.

more than once."[109] But this good approach was limited by the fact that the aunt couldn't focus exclusively on Léonie, who, once she was in a group, "has no self-control and shows herself to have unparalleled, frivolous behavior."[110]

Unable to live in community, Léonie couldn't stay at the Visitation boarding school, and the sisters were forced to send her home. Zélie, who thought that boarding-school life was the only recourse for this unstable child, was tempted to despair about her daughter. But she clung to hope in God. "I hope beyond all hope. The more I see how difficult she is, the more I persuade myself that God will not let her stay that way. I will pray so much that God will allow himself to be touched."[111]

Knowing that her maternal love might not be enough to help her daughter, she entrusted her to the best of mothers: "I plan to bring her every year to Notre-Dame de Séez, on the Feast of the Immaculate Conception."[112] For someone who didn't like pilgrimages, this was not a small sacrifice, and she even thought about taking the girl to Paray-le-Monial. "I could lose my mind over this," she said at one point.[113] Her sister upheld her wholeheartedly in this trial. Intuitively or prophetically, Marie-Dosithée was convinced that Léonie would become a saint. The parents opted for special lessons for her from two older ladies, and brought Léonie to them twice a day, which wasn't at all convenient.

Zélie started to hope again seeing her daughter prepare herself as well as she could for her first Communion in May 1875. One other small detail confirmed for Zélie that her daughter had a heart of gold despite appearances: This girl who always thought

---

[109] Letter from Sister Marie-Dosithée to Zélie Martin, February 8, 1874.
[110] *CF* 117.
[111] Ibid.
[112] Ibid.
[113] Ibid.

it a treat to go on vacations abruptly refused to go to Lisieux. The parents thought it was a whim until they discovered that Léonie was giving up her place to Céline to please her. But the situation didn't get better for all that, and in 1876 Zélie wrote: "I am coming to my end of my rope. She only does what she wants the way she wants."[114]

Even more heartbreaking for the mother, Zélie said that Léonie, who was entering adolescence, seemed to reject her completely, finding ways to contradict her and always doing the opposite of what she wanted: "I had tried by all the means I could think of to draw her to myself; everything had failed until now, and that has been the greatest sorrow of my life."[115] Zélie didn't doubt that the Lord would fulfill her hope and bring her daughter's heart to him, as we shall see.

For Louis and Zélie, the education of the children had a goal: to "raise them for heaven."[116] Most of all, they wanted holiness for their daughters. "While waiting, we need to serve God and his saints, my dear little daughters, and try to deserve to be among the number of saints."[117]

Zélie used a floral metaphor that was dear to the whole family when describing the educational method of the Martins: One needs to plow up the ground, count confidently on dew from heaven, do everything possible to cultivate it well, and then let God grow the flowers and fruits. Education was done with and for God.

Through their powerful example, more than through words, the Martin parents showed their children what the Christian

---

[114] *CF* 169.
[115] *CF* 194.
[116] *CF* 192.
[117] *CF* 110.

life is. The children saw their parents pray every day. Louis, their "king," got on his knees, and that went a long way to telling the little girls—who admired their father deeply—about God. This was the case to such an extent that one night, not seeing him say his prayers, Thérèse at the age of two, reacted sharply: "Why aren't you saying your prayers, Papa?"[118]

Heaven was so present in that home that there was no need for long talks about it—the children were saturated with it. "Léonie hears us talking about the next life so much that she talks about it too."[119] Marie later testified that her parents had a profound faith and in hearing them talk about eternity together, the daughters were disposed, as young as they were, to consider the things of this world as empty. The little girls soon imitated their parents in their zeal for souls. Zélie repeated in a letter what Pauline had written one day with a touching naiveté about the sermons she was hearing at school: they were "so beautiful, so very beautiful, that if a sinner she had in mind would hear them, he would have to convert; it would be impossible to do otherwise."[120]

The girls imitated their parents in their sacrificial attitude as well. Zélie recounted with pride how Marie endured a painful time at the dentist without squirming because she had decided to offer her suffering for the soul of her deceased grandfather. And if Marie was capable of such a sacrifice, it was because she saw her mother choose to offer all her sacrifices to the Lord for the same intention.[121]

Louis and Zélie were more than just examples of Christian life, they were both living images of God for their children.

---

[118] *CF* 130.

[119] *CF* 159.

[120] *CF* 118.

[121] See *CF* 43 for this episode.

Thérèse would move much more easily toward the Father because of having experienced a human father full of goodness and tenderness. Twice in her writing, Thérèse explained mercy and a childlike spirit to her readers by presenting them with the picture of a child committing an offense, who instead of hiding himself for fear of reprisals, throws himself into the arms of his father where he is welcomed like the prodigal son.

One of Zélie's stories gives insight into this image. One day Thérèse made believe she was sleeping and hid under her blanket when her mother tried to kiss her. Her mother was displeased about this, and she let her know it:

> Two minutes later I heard her crying and soon after, to my great surprise, she was at my side! She had gotten out of bed all by herself, had come down the stairs barefoot, hampered by a nightgown that was too long for her. Her little face was covered with tears. "Maman," she said, throwing herself at my knees, "I was bad. Forgive me!" Forgiveness was quickly given. I took my cherubim in my arms, holding her to my chest and covering her with kisses. When she saw that she had been well received, she said, "Oh! Maman, if only you wrapped me up tight like when I was little! . . ." I took the time to go find her blanket, and then I wrapped her up like when she was little. I felt like I was playing with a doll."[122]

Thérèse would act the same way with God and would be as well received. Louis and Zélie opened up a royal highway on which Thérèse would run.

The Martin parents didn't draw their educational precepts from psychology but from the Gospel, and Jesus was the reference

---

[122] *CF* 188.

point they gave their children. We can see that in the following story. Céline, four years old at the time, was playing in the street when a poor child came by and looked at her in a mocking way. "Go away," said the little Martin girl, and the other little girl said she would give her "a well-aimed blow." Zélie counseled Céline to forgive the aggressor, which seemed as scandalous to her as it did to Jesus' listeners. "You want me, Maman, to love the poor who slap me so hard it makes my cheek red?" With the unrelenting logic of the children, she declared, "I really don't like poor people!"[123] Her mother said that God wasn't pleased by that attitude because he loved the poor so much. But Céline was stubborn and left to go to bed, without doubt accompanied by her mother's prayer. The next morning, the little girl rushed up to Zélie and proudly announced: "I have a nice bouquet for the Blessed Virgin and for good Jesus. I love poor people now!"[124]

Louis and Zélie were persuaded that "it's only the first step that is costly on the path of evil or the path of good. After that, you will be swept along by the current."[125] The Martin parents accompanied their children's first steps literally and figuratively. And the first steps on the road of virtue were much more important for them than any other steps. Rather than using candy or small coins to motivate their daughters to do good, they proposed supernatural goals for them: a sinner to convert, Jesus to console. Their method was effective: among these goals, we find the pillar of Thérèse's "little way," which was "to please Jesus."

Louis and Zélie also prioritized the struggle against pride. "Keep back thy servant also from presumptuous sins," says Psalm 19:13. The Martin parents knew humility was the path to holiness and cultivated it through all possible means. Zélie's let-

---

[123] *CF* 105.
[124] Ibid.
[125] *CF* 1.

ters show her amazement about her daughters, but she didn't let them see that: "The children who are idolized by the whole world have to combat this fault [pride] more than others do if it is not reprimanded by their parents."[126] They let no conceit go by. One day Marie, who was sensitive about titles and great families, gathered some flowers from the family home and announced her desire to bring them to school. Her father, guessing her real intention, briskly reproved her that she would be saying they came from *her* property. The lesson made a deep impression.

Trained from a young age to distinguish good from bad, the Martin girls developed sensitive consciences. Marie, for example, could not fully rejoice at school for a prize she received because she was not sure of having deserved it. Although their sensitivity was good, it was tinged at times with scrupulosity. The girls were not spared from certain misguided sayings such as, "Heaven is for good children," or "If you sin, God won't love you anymore." Louis and Zélie weren't perfect parents, but we need to put these kinds of sayings in the context of an era when they were commonplace. Although they could be quite damaging in a milieu of superficial religion, they were much less traumatizing when the parental attitude demonstrated God's goodness.

Louis and Zélie were amazed as they saw the light of faith kindled in the hearts of their children: "Thérèse says her prayers like a little angel, it's wonderful!"[127] One night Zélie offered her seven-year-old Céline a small bit of chocolate, but she didn't respond. The child told her later that she was too busy "giving her heart to God."[128] Zélie was even more moved since she was convinced that "God hears the prayers of children."[129] The Martin

---

[126] *CF* 50.
[127] *CF* 177.
[128] *CF* 174.
[129] *CF* 88.

girls were raised for heaven from their conception. Zélie's union with God and the fervor of her prayers was so great whenever she was pregnant that, according to Céline, she wasn't surprised to see dispositions to piety in those children once their understanding was awakened.

The Martins were flexible in their approach to passing on their faith. "This afternoon I made Léonie come alongside me to read her some prayers, but she soon had enough and said to me, 'Maman, tell me about the life of Our Lord Jesus Christ.' I had not decided to recount it to her because it tires me out so much and I always have a sore throat. In the end I made an effort to tell her the life of Our Lord. When I got to the passion, she was overcome with tears. I was pleased to see these sentiments."[130]

Louis and Zélie guided their children toward a fervent Christian life but did so wisely. Zélie was worried to see fifteen-year-old Marie going to the 6:00 a.m. Mass every morning. She herself got up at dawn, but believed that was too early for her daughter. Marie was then going through a bit of an adolescent crisis, and Zélie felt that her counsel to prudence wouldn't be heard. She went to Sister Marie-Dosithée, who had great influence on the young girl and who succeeded in convincing her niece that she needed more sleep. But Zélie admired the piety of her oldest child. Without being forced, Marie said her Rosary every day and continued to go to Mass. Louis and Zélie knew that only God can give faith and that no one can force a child to believe, but they at least gave their daughters all the opportunities that helped implant grace in their hearts. And they did that successfully since each of the Martin girls developed a strong love for the Lord that prepared them to give him their lives.

---

[130] *CF* 88.

Some people may wonder if Louis and Zélie trained their children with the goal of making religious out of them. What future did they prepare them for through the education they gave them? The answer lies at the heart of their vision of education: Their children didn't belong to them.

The Martins believed that they were trustees of God's authority concerning their children and that the "author's rights" belonged only to him. This conviction deepened with the loss of their four little "angels." Every child was welcomed as a blessing from heaven, whatever the Martins' financial or health circumstances. The attitude of the Martins is a model for all of us: a generous acceptance of life with humble confidence in God. Boy or girl, it didn't matter to them. When her sister-in-law announced the birth of a daughter, Zélie responded, "If you are like I am, you did not grieve about this [having a girl], because I never had a minute of regret over that."[131]

Louis and Zélie did, however, long for a son who could be a priest. They admired the hands of their first little Joseph because they seemed made to hold the holy Eucharist later. But if their son had grown up, it is certain they would have left him free to choose his own path. They refused to control the arrival time of their babies or their particular futures, abandoning the arrival times to the Lord and the futures to the freedom of their children. At the beginning of their marriage, however, they were not in that place. Louis and Zélie prayed that since they themselves could not be religious, that all their children would become religious. It was a naive prayer, colored by their earlier disappointment about their own vocations. Their prayer would be different several years later after they experienced a conversion about their perspective on their vocation and an increasingly radical abandonment to God's will.

---

[131] *CF* 59.

When Zélie began to suspect that Marie was thinking about religious life, she wrote to Pauline: "Don't say anything to her about this because she will think it is what I want, and I really do not want it unless it is God's will. As long as she follows the vocation that he gives her, I will be content."[132] Marie, meanwhile, felt so little encouraged by her parents to enter religious life that she reproached them one day, weeping, because they had bought her a beautiful dress; she thought they "were dressing her like a young girl that we wanted to marry off at all costs, and certainly we would be the reason that she would be asked for in marriage."[133] Zélie encouraged her daughters to go out and spend time with young people their age. One day when Marie was invited to a meeting of young girls, Sister Marie-Dosithée was shocked. Zélie reacted with her normal good sense: "So she [Marie] needs to be shut up in a cloister? . . . In everything that the 'holy girl' says to us, we take it or leave it."[134]

Louis and Zélie wanted only the holiness of their daughters, whatever their state in life. At the end of her life Zélie had an inkling about the vocational direction of her two oldest daughters and said that she would be very happy to see them become religious, but at the same time that it "would not be without pain"[135] to have them leave home. She, but not Louis, was spared that pain of separation. The passing of time would show the blossoming of the five Martin daughters in their religious vocations, choices that cannot be limited to a strictly human interpretation. We can hardly put aside the divine origin for what each of them always perceived as a call of love from God.

Louis and Zélie gave their children great freedom, as they did their Creator, and instead served them.

---

[132] *CF* 147.
[133] *CF* 161.
[134] *CF* 173.
[135] *CF* 163.

Chapter 5

THE MARTIN ENTERPRISE

The Martins ran two businesses from 1858 to 1870. First, there was Louis's watchmaking and jewelry shop on the first floor of the family home on Rue du Pont-Neuf. The family home was not in the central part of the city, but Louis had a regular clientele who appreciated his talent and his honesty. He made and repaired watches and clocks and also sold a few pieces of jewelry. Starting in 1863 he helped his wife who was more and more overwhelmed by her lace-making. In 1870, he closed his shop to dedicate himself to her completely. It was no small thing, especially at that time, for a husband to leave his own professional work to devote himself to his wife's endeavors.

Since the beginning, in fact, the volume of Zélie's work was on the increase. What exactly did it involve? Father Piat explains: "Lace is made using a pattern created on vellum strips that are roughly seven by nine inches and are perforated with the design that is being reproduced. The strips are lined with linen. High quality, extremely delicate flax threads are used. Once the pattern is executed, each piece passes from hand to hand according to the number of stitches required. . . . Then one must detach each piece, cut off the useless threads, repair the inevitable rips, and then proceed to the assembly of the pieces. It's a delicate task . . . with almost imperceptible needles and thinner and thinner threads."[136]

---

[136] *HF*, p. 29.

Zélie assembled the pieces herself, even though she hired one or two assemblers at the end of her career. She grouped the orders, obtained the necessary material for those who worked at home, and supervised the transfer of pieces from one person to another. And she coordinated and corrected everything. Louis, starting in 1863, took care of the sales and dealing with clients, a job that Zélie had earlier consigned to another firm. He went to Paris regularly to do business with other shops, and he took orders, bought the material, and made the deliveries. He did the bookkeeping and occasionally even picked up a needle himself.

The Martins employed at least nine workers and paid them immediately, since the least delay seemed a true injustice to Louis and Zélie. Zélie met with them on Thursdays when they brought her the piece of lace they had sewn and left with new work to do. Thursday was a particularly active day since Zélie often had a baby in her arms and another little one running around. This system functioned well, however, since the workers played at being nannies, to the great delight of the little ones.

Zélie's employees liked her very much. One of them, Mrs. Commin, said Zélie was a very just person, good to her workers, courageous, and hardworking—a saint. If one of the workers became sick, Zélie would visit her on Sunday and provide for her needs if necessary. She couldn't bring herself to dismiss a bad employee. Miss Irma, her dressmaker, not only did her work badly, but she also lost her temper if Zélie made the least remark. Pragmatic Louis didn't want to keep her on, especially since they paid her a lot. His wife tried to intervene with him, but at first she obeyed and hired a replacement. She couldn't resist Irma's tears when she came to ask forgiveness, though, and ended up with two dressmakers when she only needed one.

Zélie wrote a letter to Isidore as he was getting ready to open a pharmacy in Lisieux, and we can sense the reality of her personal experience: "I pity you, my poor friend. You are going to enter a life full of misery, worries, and work. You really need to have courage and patience because that is not the end of it. You will be working as much as the Trappists do, but the reward will be far less."[137] In fact, Louis and Zélie had difficulty carrying the workload; they worked as much as the children allowed during the day and often "extended the days with the help of a lamp"[138] until late at night. At the busiest times, Zélie was up from 4:30 a.m. until 11:00 p.m. This tireless woman concluded: "I am obligated to work much too much. I am very unhappy about that, and I would like to have some rest before dying."[139] However, she also felt "the worse things are, the better I do!"[140]

Zélie understood the problems of being the head of an enterprise subject to the risks of fashion and the economy. "It's this headache of Alençon lace that makes my life hard. When I have too many orders I'm a slave in the worst kind of slavery. When things don't go well and I find myself 20,000 francs in debt and have to send workers I had such a hard time finding to other lace firms, I have something to be worried about, and I have had nightmares about it!"[141] Given her anxious nature, this was a real trial for her. Her letters seem to show her buried under a mountain of orders, although weeks later she could write: "My business is going badly, very badly; it could not be going worse. I definitely believe that I am at the end of my reign."[142] This false prediction shows up occasionally in her writing.

Although Zélie complained about her work, she liked it very much. She took a rare outing to distract herself, but, bored with

---

[137] *CF* 18.
[138] *CF* 22.
[139] *CF* 163.
[140] *CF* 118.
[141] *CF* 15.
[142] *CF* 32.

the experience, she wrote, "To tell the truth, I really am not happy unless I am seated at my window assembling my lace pieces."[143] That was even more true the day she wrote that comment because she had good company—she was pregnant with Thérèse. Zélie preferred a simple life working next to her husband and her children.

And she gave herself completely to her work and her family. She even said the Lord invited her to keep nothing for herself and that all her time should be given away. She made that point to her brother with some humor:

> I must say that I do not have much luck. Every time I plan an outing, a mishap occurs. I have often noticed that, so I have given up on any kind of relaxation, and I don't want to hear any more talk about it. The nicest outing I ever had was the one in Trouville. How did it end? Right at the moment that I started to enjoy it, we received a wire that made us have to change all our plans. I am sure that if I returned there, the sea would engulf me. So I said good-bye to Trouville, good-bye for good to having any rest.[144]

God doesn't condemn rest and relaxation, but Zélie's path of sacrifice was a different path. Zélie wanted to be a saint, and God offered her a path of sanctification that was suited to her. Her letters over the course of the years are impressive. She was always giving, whether to her family, to her work, to the poor. She often said she was sick of being fatigued, but she responded actively to the constant demands from others. Her daughter Thérèse later wrote, "To love means to give everything and to give one-

---

[143] *CF* 82.
[144] *CF* 122.

self completely,"[145] and that is how Zélie loved her husband, her children, her clients, her workers, and all those who knocked on her door. She, of course, suffered from always being hemmed in and didn't hide that, but she regretted nothing, feeling that she was only doing her duty like the unworthy servant in the Gospel (see Luke 17:10).

The only vacations Zélie allowed herself were trips to Lisieux about every two years. Those were joyful times. The girls visited with their cousins, and Zélie's well-loved brother and sister-in-law planned entertainment and outings for them. The only cloud on these happy occasions was Louis's absence since he had to stay to manage the shop and look after the youngest children. As for him, he had his own vacations—an annual pilgrimage or a short retreat.

Each day Zélie surrendered her affairs into God's hands a little bit more, and she ended up having a faith that was liberating: "I was like you [Isidore] when I started my lace business in Alençon. I made myself sick over it; now I am much more reasonable. I am less concerned and have resigned myself to the troublesome events that occur and that can happen to me. I tell myself that God permits this, and then I don't think about it any more."[146] Even if the risks of the business were still trials, she nevertheless recognized the hand of Providence in the operation: "God, who is a good Father and never gives his children more than they can bear, has lightened the burden, and the lace-making has slowed down."[147] And she acknowledged, "I always work with hope."[148] Zélie could have said, with St. Ignatius of Loyola, "Pray as if ev-

---

[145] *PN* 54, stanza 22.
[146] *CF* 26.
[147] *CF* 34.
[148] *CF* 44.

erything depended on God, and work as if everything depended on you."

Once when Isidore encountered some difficulties with his pharmacy, Zélie wrote him a letter that gives insight into her perspective about work:

> My sister has told me a lot about your business. She thinks that you should have a representative in several cities. As for me, I think that is attempting the impossible. I told her not to rack her brains over that, and there is only one thing to do: pray to God, since neither she nor I can help you in any other way. But God, who is never hampered, will pull us through when he thinks we have suffered enough, and then you will know that it is neither you nor your abilities but only God, as is the case for me with my Alençon lace. That conviction is very beneficial; I've experienced it myself.
>
> You know that all of us tend toward pride, and I often notice that those who have made their fortune are for the most part unbearably self-congratulatory. I'm not saying that I have gotten to that point, or you either, but we could have been more or less sullied by that pride; and it's certain that constant prosperity distances people from God. He never led his chosen ones down that path initially; they had already previously gone through the crucible of suffering for purification. You will say that I am preaching, although that is not my intention. I think about these things often and I am merely sharing them with you. So call it a sermon if you like!"[149]

---

[149] *CF* 81.

With her usual humor and liveliness, Zélie was speaking from experience.

Because of hard work and trust in God, Louis and Zélie ended up with a small fortune. Zélie attributed that success in particular to their respect for Sunday, the Lord's Day. In vain their friends and even Louis's confessor tried to convince them to work on Sunday. Sunday was a market day in the area around Rue du Pont-Neuf, so it was a day of crowds. Louis could have done good business if he had opened his shop, and he did have children to feed, after all. And Zélie, when she had too much work, could have gotten ahead by working on Sunday rather than wearing herself out working late at night during the week. But these trusting Christians, who had put all their affairs in God's hands, didn't see how they would gain by breaking his commandment, which they respected as his children. "Remember the sabbath day, to keep it holy," the Book of Exodus says. "Six days you shall labor, and do all your work; but the seventh day is a sabbath to the Lord your God; in it you shall not do any work" (20:8-10).

Honoring the Lord's Day implied many things for the Martins. In order not to cooperate with other people working that day, Louis avoided taking the train and Zélie avoided doing any shopping on Sunday. "Very often I admire Louis's scruples and I say to myself, 'There is a man who never tried to make a fortune.' . . . I cannot attribute the prosperity he enjoys to anything but a special blessing that is the fruit of his filial observance of Sunday."[150] She also predicted a similar blessing for her brother, who at that time was having trouble making ends meet but who, like Louis, scrupulously respected Sunday rest.

Sunday, however, was less a time of rest for the Martin spouses than it was a holy day. They went to the first Mass and received Communion, then to High Mass, and sometimes to a third Mass for more grace. This wasn't extraordinary in that era.

---

[150] *CF* 140.

A good lunch would reunite the whole family, and then, if the children were napping or playing quietly, Zélie would start her correspondence while Louis read. After vespers and a nice walk, everyone returned to church for the Exposition of the Blessed Sacrament. Time together in the evening was followed by family prayer, which concluded the day—a day that ended for Zélie only when her correspondence was done.

With their fortune assured, Louis and Zélie could have slowed down the pace of their work beginning in 1872. They could even have sold their lace business and enjoyed a peaceful retirement. They didn't do that for two main reasons. First, and this is to their credit, they didn't want their employees to lose their jobs. The second reason is more ambiguous: Zélie seemed to have a scrupulous concern to ensure the financial future for her daughters. Her exaggerated attitude could be explained by the lack of money that she had experienced in her family as a child. Marie came to despise her mother's job, which she also perceived as slavery, and it must be said that Zélie's choice to keep working until her final days does raise questions.

Louis and Zélie never worked to amass a fortune, however, nor did they do so to climb any social ladder. Their only goal was to be able to educate their children and open doors for them: "Their father and I have to work to earn a dowry for them; if not, when they are grown, they will not be pleased with us!"[151] Several years later she said: "It would be foolish of me to leave my work since I have five children that I need to help get started in life. I need to do as much as I can for them."[152]

Louis and Zélie weren't materialists. When Marie, as an adolescent, began to envy the lovely apartments of her rich friends, Zélie wrote: "Marie is dreaming of having other things [than

---

[151] *CF* 31.
[152] *CF* 152.

what we have]. If she did have other things, she would feel the emptiness perhaps even more. As for me, I imagine that if I was in a magnificent château surrounded by all that someone could want on earth, the emptiness would be greater than if I were by myself alone in a small attic, forgetting the world or being forgotten by it."[153] According to Zélie, only God can fill us up.

The Martins knew they couldn't serve God and money and had a particularly balanced attitude about finances, neither despising nor idolizing money. They knew that in their vocation as laypeople and parents, holy poverty didn't consist in having nothing, but rather in using money in a reasonable way for oneself and being generous to others. Unlike their friends, once Louis and Zélie made their fortune, they didn't change their lifestyle, which remained simple. Their linen was always clean; their furniture was of good quality without being expensive; they ate ordinary food but ate better on feast days or when guests came. However, they forbad unnecessary expenses and anything too luxurious, often repeating from *The Imitation of Christ*, "Having this world's goods in abundance is not man's happiness; a modest share is sufficient."[154]

Louis was responsible for the finances. He decided how to distribute the budget to cover ongoing bills, investments, and gifts. Zélie gave him her input and felt free to "pester" him at times on an issue. After the war in 1870, for example, she urged him to sell part of his land bank shares. Louis knew it was an unwise move, but he gave in to his wife out of generosity because the liquidated funds would allow them to help the Guérin family who was having difficulty because of the war. At the same time, Zélie didn't conceal that she had no talent for finance. She therefore trusted her husband for the management of the family portfolio. For minor expenses, like clothes for the girls, she

---

[153] *CF* 150.

[154] See *The Imitation of Christ*, 1, 22.

was the one who had the purse strings. Louis would tease his wife freely on this subject. One day when she had to buy a new wardrobe for the children, she wrote: "In a word, I'm having to buy clothes every day! Your father says shopping is a passion of mine! It does no good to tell him that I have no choice since he has trouble believing that. But he trusts me and knows very well that I will not ruin him!"[155]

In business Louis and Zélie were honest and preferred to be swindled rather than shortchange anyone even just a little bit. When Zélie's father had refused to pay a contractor because he considered himself wronged, the man came to collect the money from his children. Not only did Louis and Zélie settle the issue immediately without any discussion, but they also didn't want Isidore to take part in the contractor's reimbursement. "My husband said to me, 'I insist that Isidore does not pay his share because he has treated you so well.' I tell this story to show you how good Louis is."[156] Louis sold his watchmaking shop to his nephew in 1870 for the same price he had paid for it twenty years earlier. Taking into account inflation and the fact that a business appreciates in value from year to year, it was a generous gesture.

The Martins never stopped loaning money to those around them: to Isidore for his business ventures, to other businesses they were working with, to particular people who were in need, to stores that were threatened with having to close . . . all without charging any interest. They were generous creditors. When the war threatened them with the loss of everything, not only did they refuse to collect anything from their debtors, who were in difficulty themselves, but they also had sympathy for them.

Even during times when money was not abundant, there was always something in the family budget for the poor—for charitable works and for the Church. Was there a flood that occurred

---

[155] *CF* 143.
[156] *CF* 77.

in Lisieux? The Martins immediately loosened up funds to come to the assistance of the disaster victims. "Give, always give, and make some people happy," Louis wrote in 1885.[157] That could have been his motto.

---

[157] *CF* 226.

Chapter 6

A MISSIONARY COUPLE

Louis and Zélie's beatification took place on a significant date, October 19, 2008—World Mission Day. The Martins' precise mission was to transmit life and to educate their children in the faith, and we have seen how they succeeded at that, but they can be called missionaries in a much broader sense.

Louis and Zélie believed that every person they encountered was sent to them by Providence. If there was a need, they would help someone as much as they could, imitating Christ who healed the sick before talking to them about the kingdom of God.

They didn't limit their charity to a percentage set apart in the budget and sent to charitable associations. Instead, Louis and Zélie also gave themselves, even when it was inconvenient. Examples of this abound.

One day Louis came across a homeless family in the street. He brought them home, and Zélie fed them and talked with them while her husband got busy trying to find a job for the father. After regaining a normal life, thanks to the Martins' care, the family sent them a short verse for the birth of Thérèse in gratitude: "Little bud that has just emerged, you will be a rose some day!"[158] It couldn't have been better said.

Louis wasn't afraid, on several occasions, to separate men in knife fights, and he was an excellent swimmer who saved several

---

[158] *HF*, pp. 124-125.

people from drowning. He was an on-the-spot fireman when the fire alarm rang, and one day he saved an elderly lady from flames. Knowing his propensity to heroic actions, his family worried when this punctual man was late, wondering what potentially dangerous adventure he had gotten himself into.

Spotting an unfortunate beggar who was holding out his hand unsuccessfully in a train station, Louis took off his own hat, filled it with a generous amount of money and went around to the other travelers, begging in the place of the beggar. And he didn't limit his assistance just to the "presentable poor." When he saw a drunken workman falling down in the street one day and people walking by and turning away from him, Louis picked him up and took him home. He returned the next day to talk to the man to try to persuade him not to start drinking again.

Zélie was just as charitable. Céline later said that just like her father, her mother had great concern for the poor in whatever distress they were in, she was never afraid of the trouble it meant for her, and she never set boundaries to her generosity. Her mother often took unfortunate people into the Martin home, and also gave them money.

One day on the train, Zélie saw a woman with her children, weighed down with bags. Not only did she help her during the journey, but she also accompanied her to her home, not returning to Rue Saint-Blaise until midnight. When Louis came to meet her at the train station, he unloaded the packages of the other woman and found himself perplexed at having to hold a baby in his arms. "I told him I had found a little girl and I was bringing her home," she said to her sister-in-law. "He didn't look too happy."[159]

Zélie's upright, generous character was evident in another situation. Léonie, after her failure as a boarder at the Visitation Monastery, was taking special lessons in 1875 with two religious

---

[159] *CF* 141.

who were living in Alençon. They were raising a child, Armandine, and frequently solicited gifts for her. Fairly quickly Zélie suspected that the little girl was malnourished, so every day she had Léonie bring her something good to eat. She even proposed to the women that she could take charge of her meals. But then she discovered that Armandine was also being mistreated: "I was so indignant that I didn't even want to take time to eat."[160] She went looking for the child's mother right away. Zélie wrote to the two religious to inform them of her disgust, but she was dealing with two manipulators, one of whom turned up at the Martins' home.

> She arrived with an amiability that I cannot describe to you. She assured me, in trying to cry, that if I had thought her a saint, she wanted to humble herself before me and undeceive me. This went on for about a quarter of an hour in the same vein. I answered, "But, Sister, you speak the language of a saint, and no saints have spoken better than you have." Her face was beaming. She thought she had won me over with her humility and that I was going to throw myself at her feet. . . . I continued, "So, Sister, do you repent of the things you made that child suffer?" Her face then took on a ferocious expression and she declared that none of my accusations were true. I answered her coldly, without becoming angry, that everything I had accused her of in my letter was the truth, and she left, holding back her fury as well as she could."[161]

Zélie wasn't deceived by a religious habit. A habit does not make a monk, and she learned that these religious had never been nuns. Chased out of their last parish, they had been wear-

---

[160] CF 128.
[161] Ibid.

ing the habit illegally and were using Armandine to ensure their own comfort. Unfortunately, Zélie was the only one to see clearly through their ruse, and the two fake nuns, playing the role of persecuted saints, began to spread the worst rumors about her. Armandine's mother, forewarned, then came to Zélie and told her: "I just came from the Sisters. I grabbed my child and tried to take her away. As I got to the doorway, they opened their windows and started shouting, 'Help! Stop the abductor!' A crowd gathered and four strong men got together and grabbed the little one out of my arms, as the Sisters meanwhile were vomiting a flood of offensive sayings against you, Madame, and against me!"[162]

After a last attempt at trying to reason with them, a night of insomnia, and a long prayer, Zélie resolved to go to the police station, accompanied by Louis and the poor mother. That was a hard step for Zélie who wasn't at ease in public and didn't like conflicts. The sisters had earlier terrorized Armandine to keep her quiet and had made her drink alcohol so that she looked relaxed. They put on their best front with the police commissioner who was beginning to take their side. Zélie believed that she might even be put in prison: "I saw myself at the point of being accused of deception and if they had bled all my limbs, I believe that not one drop of blood would have come out!"[163]

She then had the inspired idea of asking to be heard apart with Armandine. Freed from the gaze of her torturers, the child affirmed all that she had been subjected to. Zélie was relieved, and the fake sisters, to everyone's indignation, exploded in a hysterical attack against Zélie. The commissioner intervened, and the affair ended for the best with the child being returned to her mother.

Everyone was edified by Zélie's behavior, but she saw less her work than God's work in all this because she had ardently

---

[162] Ibid.
[163] *CF* 129.

prayed, and said, "God, I believe, had his hand in this affair."[164] After this the two women spread slander about the Martins and despite her efforts, Zélie couldn't stop Armandine from turning against her.

Zélie concluded in faith: "It must be admitted I don't have any luck, and that on a human level it's not encouraging to try to do good. If only this miserable affair would earn me a merciful gaze from heaven, I would consider myself adequately compensated."[165] By nature Zélie liked to have her efforts acknowledged and was sensitive about being thanked. She said that she often received no thanks from the people she helped, but rather than becoming embittered she profited from it by turning to heaven. After all, she was working for God and not for people's gratitude.

Louis and Zélie knew that the most valuable help they could bring to a situation was more spiritual than material in nature. The salvation of souls was their priority, and prayer was their best weapon. Religious indifference saddened them, so they had no problem testifying to their faith. When Louis was invited one day to a spiritual event [some kind of paranormal experience] where tables rotated, he went, but not out of curiosity. Pressured to join in, he categorically refused and began to pray within himself. The table didn't move an inch that night, and some blamed him for that, while others, touched by his attitude, learned a lesson from that event.

In particular, they had their hearts set on the conversion of sinners on the threshold of death. They knew the stakes. When they heard Isidore talk about a young man who was going to die unrepentant, the whole family got involved. They prayed, had a Mass said, entrusted the situation to St. Joseph, and Zélie made

---

[164] Ibid.
[165] *CF* 146.

a novena—and the young man asked for the sacraments a few hours before his death. This wasn't an isolated case. The Martin spouses worked together to procure the last rites for anyone in their area who was dying. Louis often arranged for the sacrament for the dying to be brought to a home whose doors his charity had long ago opened.

When a neighboring lady who didn't practice her faith was about to die, Zélie was upset: "My God, how sad to see a home without religion! How awful death must seem! . . . I hope God will accept this woman out of pity; she was so badly brought up that she could be excused."[166] Zélie ensured that Extreme Unction was administered and took the dying woman's two children into her home. And her prayers were answered. "Fernande [the daughter] told me that her mother had prayed right to the end. The good Lord must have shown her mercy."[167] Zélie kept the orphans in her prayers, and Louis took care of all the death notifications.

By their witness, their prayers, and their actions, Louis and Zélie announced the good news to those they encountered. But their missionary impulse led them even further as they joined in the intentions of the universal Church. Every year Louis gave a generous gift to the Pontifical Missionary Societies, and he and Zélie attentively followed the missionary adventures of the era. They participated through prayer—Zélie, for example, was enrolled in a prayer association for the conversion of the people in the East.

They had dreamed of a son not just to be a priest but to be a missionary. God granted that missionary desire, but in his typical way—that is, in an unexpected way—beyond all hope in making their daughter the patron of missions.

---

[166] *CF* 145.
[167] *CF* 146.

Chapter 7

THE TIME OF TRIALS

Perhaps because of the onset of her cancer, Zélie could no longer nurse her babies from 1866 on. The Martins were then obliged to hire wet nurses, but it wasn't easy to find a woman who could nurse the babies and take good care of them. The newspapers at that time frequently recounted stories of wet nurses who let children die. And so Louis and Zélie engaged in an intensive search to discover that "rare pearl." They ended up finding Rose Taillé, a farm lady who lived in Sémallé about five miles from Alençon. She took care of the two Josephs, Céline, and Thérèse.

The distance was not prohibitive for the parents who were intent on their children's survival and well-being. They often traveled the ten miles, and even twenty miles, when a child was sick. On one such occasion, Zélie recounted: "You can imagine that it didn't take me long to get dressed and be on my way to the countryside on the coldest night and in spite of the snow and ice. I didn't ask my husband to come with me because I didn't feel afraid. I would have gone through the forest by myself, but he wouldn't let me go without him."[168]

The separation from their babies was heartbreaking, and we can imagine Zélie's feelings the day Thérèse came to visit from Sémallé and didn't seem to recognize her mother; she stopped crying only when she was back in the arms of her wet nurse.

---

[168] *CF* 21.

These painful separations prefigured a period of more intense separation. In the space of three years, the Martins would bury five people: Zélie's father and four of their children.

The first death they had to face was that of their little Joseph, born in September 1866. This first boy had been the joy of his parents, and Zélie was already picturing herself sewing Alençon lace for the future alb of this priest. But despite the good care of Rose Taillé, he died five months later from enteritis.

The only document we have about this terrible event is the response of Sister Marie-Dosithée at the announcement of his death, a response that only Christians of the Martins' stature could hear: "Dear sister, how can I comfort you? . . . God gave him to us and has taken him away. Blessed be his name! This morning at communion as I was praying to Our Lord that he would let us keep this little one, whom we wanted to raise only for his glory and for the acquisition of souls, it seemed to me I heard this answer interiorly, that he wanted the first fruits but that he would give you another child later who would be just like what we desire."[169]

Seeming to be an answer to this prayer, a second boy, also named Joseph, was born in December 1867. He too needed to be sent to the wet nurse, and died in August the following year. Sister Marie-Dosithée again wrote, "It is the Master of the dove-house who came to take your little dove to bring him to paradise, so let us acquiesce with all our strength to his will."[170]

There was no respite for the grieving parents because less than ten days later, Zélie's father died, too. She had never been away from him for long and was deeply attached to the gruff but good man. She wrote at that point, "My heart aches with sorrow,

---

[169] Letter from Sister Marie-Dosithée to Zélie Martin, February 15, 1867 (see Archives of Carmel in Lisieux).

[170] *HF*, p. 61.

but at the same time it is filled with heavenly consolation."[171] Her
reaction clarifies the lovely text from Madeleine Delbrêl: "Death
is known all over again at each definitive detachment from loved
ones. Even when faith and hope are united and our love for them
affirms our joy of knowing them to be gone home, we are left
behind with our empty flesh that protests, our flesh that seems
to have had a large piece of itself killed off at this horror of earth,
of the darkness and cold that made even Jesus cry."[172] Zélie described it this way:

> Saturday I was looking everywhere for my father. It
> seemed that I was going to find him; I could not believe I
> was separated from him. . . . Yesterday I went to the cem-
> etery. If anyone would have seen me they would have said,
> "That is the most indifferent person in the world." I was
> on my knees at the foot of his grave and I could not pray.
> A few steps farther on, I knelt by the graves of my two
> little angels; I showed the same apparent indifference.
> . . . I was walking down the same road that I had walked
> five weeks ago with my little baby and my father. I could
> not tell you all that I felt. I was not paying attention to
> anything going on around me. I looked at the spots where
> my father used to sit and stood there with my mind blank.
> Never in my life had I ever felt such heartache. Returning
> home, I could not eat. It seemed to me that any kind of
> new misfortune would leave me unfeeling.[173]

A month later a new separation occurred: Louis and Zélie sent their two oldest daughters to boarding school at the

[171] *CF* 38.
[172] Madeleine Delbrêl, *Alcide* (Paris: Editions du Seuil, 1968), p. 86.
[173] *CF* 39.

Visitation Monastery. All these trials affected Zélie's health: headaches, toothaches, insomnia, and loss of appetite. She went through episodes of depression. She looked so bad at that point that many predicted an early reunion with her beloved departed ones. The response from the hardworking mother was, "I don't have time to die; I have too much work right now!"[174] In fact, managing their household left Louis and Zélie no time to dwell on their situation, which in any case wouldn't have been in line with their temperaments.

Eighteen months later, death came knocking once again at the Martins' door, carrying off their adorable little Hélène at the age of five on February 22, 1870. She had been languishing for several months, and then had difficulty breathing, dying suddenly. According to Zélie:

> She [Hélène] was looking at a bottle of medicine that the doctor had given her, and she wanted to drink it, saying that when she had drunk it all she would be healed. Then toward 9:45 she said to me, "Yes, very soon I will be healed, yes, right away. . . ." At the same moment while I was holding her, her little head fell on my shoulder, her eyes closed, and five minutes later she was gone. . . . That left an impression on me that I will never forget. I was not expecting such an abrupt ending nor did my husband. When he came back in and saw his little girl had died, he began sobbing and crying out, "My little Hélène! My little Hélène!" Then together we offered her to God. . . . Before her burial I spent the night beside this poor little darling; she was more beautiful in death than in life. I was the one who dressed her and put her in the casket. I thought I would die doing it, but I did not want

---

[174] *CF* 42.

others touching her. . . . I will grieve all my life over little Hélène![175]

That is what she would in fact do, just like Louis who up until his last illness would repeat the verse from François-René Châteaubriand, "Oh! Who will bring my Hélène back to me?"[176] Zélie's suffering was compounded by the stinging grief of guilt. All her life Zélie blamed herself for some simple food she had fed little Hélène to please her that she later thought had been fatal for her. "I blame myself completely for everything," Zélie said.[177] She had the same experience with each serious illness of her nursing children: "I don't know what to do or how to handle it. I'm afraid of not giving the child what is needed; it is a continual death for me. Someone would have to walk that path to know what torment really is. I do not know if purgatory is worse than this."[178]

Another anguish seized Zélie about Hélène's death: She was bitterly angry with herself for not having given the child the chance to go to confession before her death. Could her daughter still enter heaven in that state? The idea that her child could be suffering in purgatory was unbearable for her. In her torment, she turned to the statue of the Blessed Mother. She felt she received an immediate answer, murmured by a gentle voice, that Hélène was there in heaven, next to the Blessed Mother.

Grief over Hélène's death was without doubt the most painful sorrow for the Martins, and this time Zélie had a hard time withstanding the blow:

---

[175] *CF* 53.
[176] A verse from a song in the novel *The Last of the Abencerrajes* (1826), by François-Rene Châteaubriand.
[177] *CF* 52.
[178] *CF* 89.

As for me I am not confined to my bed, but I am not doing very well at all. To be more precise, I often have a fever every day. I'm not suffering from it that much, but I have a constant headache and am generally weak. I have no energy, I cannot work quickly, and I have no heart to do any work. Sometimes I think that I am drifting away quietly like my little Hélène. I can assure you that I hardly care about my own life. Since I lost that child I have experienced a fervent desire to see her again. However, the children who remain need me, and because of them I pray that God will give me more years on earth."[179]

Once more Zélie pulled herself together for the good of her family, especially since she was pregnant again.

The first little Thérèse was born later that year on August 16, 1870. Zélie was still unable to nurse the baby, and Rose Taillé was not available. After a desperate search, Louis heard many good things about a wet nurse in the city. They left their child with her, but the baby began dying little by little. The Martin parents didn't discover soon enough that the woman was underfeeding their child, and when they did find out, it was too late. After a few days, when she seemed to be recovering, the baby was in agony, suffering horribly on her mother's knees. Zélie's heart was broken. She wrote to her brother, "I could die too!"[180] Louis and Zélie once again had no time to dwell on this death, since one month later a new trial awaited them: war.

Facing so many crosses, what was the reaction of these parents? Their strength in facing their griefs was impressive, but they were not heroes: "My God!" Zélie exclaimed, "How weary I am of

---

[179] *CF* 54.
[180] *CF* 60.

suffering! I have not got a dime's worth of courage!"[181] Zélie's anguish intensified in fearing the loss of her other children: "I have already had many torments about this child [Céline]. I feel that I am wearing out. I have the impression that I will not live a long time. During the six days that I was taking care of the little one, I had a fever every day. It was not so much from weariness as from fear."[182] Céline also had symptoms of enteritis and, even more serious, was experiencing a period of fatigue that painfully evoked Hélène's last illness.

Their philosophy of life reflected these trials: "So, you see, my dear sister, the happiest people are only the least unhappy. The wisest thing, the simplest thing, in all this is to resign oneself to God's will and to prepare ahead of time to carry one's cross as bravely as possible."[183] This is the realism of a woman whose experience had not made her bitter but had led her to focus on the essential.

Their sorrow didn't make them insensitive to the pain of others, it quickened their compassion. When Isidore and his wife lost their little Paul, Louis and Zélie wept with them as though he had been theirs. Louis "was very sensitive about your pain and talks about it constantly. We go over in our minds all the suffering and anxiety that your poor wife had to go through for six months and lament the sad outcome."[184] With all the gentleness and depth that her experience had given her, Zélie comforted her sister-in-law.

How were Louis and Zélie able to bear all this grief without bitterness or rebellion? The answer is found in their deep faith. Through trial after trial, they ended up working out their own theology of suffering. Louis and Zélie, in humility, knew their place with respect to God: They were not the masters of life and death. Zélie said that these children were recalled by God, that

---

[181] *CF* 41.

[182] *CF* 48.

[183] *CF* 51.

[184] *CF* 71.

is, called by God: "God is the Master, and he did not have to ask my permission."[185] Children are a gift and not something owed to parents. Grief helped the Martin parents grow in humility, and so after the death of the two Josephs, the couple stopped asking God for a future priest and asked for nothing more than the fulfillment of his will.

The Lord "took" their children to himself, but the Martins, with heroic submission, also gave or offered them to him. Jesus said, "No one takes it [my life] from me, but I lay it down of my own accord" (Jn 10:18). It was with that same freedom that they offered God what was more precious to them than their own lives, the lives of their children. Thérèse would later think of Mary at the foot of the cross as a priest offering the Holy Sacrifice on the altar. This is also the way Louis and Zélie appear from their time of agony and the death of their children. They offered God their children in their suffering, but they were full of trust and, paradoxically, the joy of salvation, just like Mary at Calvary. In their trials, they recognized God's hand as only those who have fully surrendered their lives to him can. Suffering and death were no longer absurd but, as their daughter would later say, "blows of love."[186]

It can be hard to imagine what kind of faith it takes to enter so fully into God's perspective. God allows trials, knows how to make us come out of them, and never ceases accompanying his children. That is the theology of the Martin suffering that they fully lived and incarnated, and it is none other than the Church's theology. Zélie summarized it after a new grief: "Meanwhile, my dear friend, let us not murmur against God, for he is the Master; he can let us suffer a lot for our own good, but his help and his grace will never let us down."[187] All of that suffering didn't in the least diminish Zélie's trust in her good Father.

---

[185] *CF* 65.
[186] *LT* 94, Letter from Thérèse to Céline Martin, July 14, 1889.
[187] *CF* 71.

Reflecting on this sad period, Zélie said: "God never gives more than people can bear. . . . I was, however, overwhelmed by work and worries of every kind, but I had this firm confidence of being sustained from on high."[188] In addition to their confidence in the goodness of God and his Providence, the hope that their deceased children were in heaven sustained them: "This child [their first Thérèse] is happy and that comforts me."[189] Zélie became outraged whenever she heard people say that it would have been better not to have had the children than to have lost them: "I didn't think that the sorrows and worries could ever be weighed against the eternal happiness of my children."[190] Bitter tears for Louis and Zélie, but joy for their children, that is the consolation of generous parents.

With their little "angels" they experienced the communion of saints in heaven and on earth. Five weeks after the death of the first little Joseph, Zélie felt inspired to have him pray for Hélène who had a dangerous ear infection that the doctors couldn't cure. The next day, her ear was perfectly healed. Louis and Zélie began the habit of invoking their children in heaven and obtained many graces through their intercession. At the Martins' home, the death of children was not a forbidden topic. Those children were still living members of the family who participated in family life, and the Martins talked about them, spoke to them, and awaited the joy of seeing them in heaven. Thérèse said that during her adolescence she looked to her four brothers and sisters in heaven for help, and they never let her down.

We can understand how Zélie, despite all the sorrow of her grief, could speak without pretense about "the joy of having a child in heaven."[191] Louis and Zélie never failed to witness to this

---

[188] *CF* 65.
[189] *CF* 61.
[190] *CF* 72.
[191] Ibid.

wonderful reality to those around them, but with the sensitivity of experienced people. "You can see, my dear sister, that it is a great good to have a child in heaven, but it is not less painful for our human nature to lose the child; these are the great sorrows of our lives."[192]

As Zélie said, "There is always joy alongside the pain."[193] The Martins didn't turn in on their sorrow and knew how to benefit from the joy they gave each other and from the joy their children gave them. The atmosphere in their family home, despite trials, was always cheerful.

On July 16, 1870, France, humiliated by the Prussians and worried about their desire to dominate Europe, declared war on Prussia. But the French army was poor, ill prepared, badly commanded, and outnumbered by the Prussians. It was a disaster. On September 2, the Emperor Napoleon III signed the surrender in Sedan and lost his throne, but a new French Republic was proclaimed and continued to fight. For the Martins, at a time when this political regime still seemed similar to the bloody, anticlerical Reign of Terror during the French Revolution, it was not good news.

The Prussian army progressively invaded France and ended up arriving near Alençon. On November 22, the army appeared at the outskirts of the city, and the Martins witnessed a sad spectacle similar to the one that occurred seventy years later in World War II: half of the city left as refugees toward the west, while the others hid their goods and scuffled with the army.

At first Zélie reacted very calmly to the prospect of an invasion. After all the losses she had been through, nothing frightened her. She even told her relatives in Lisieux some humorous episodes. One neighbor had hidden his valuables in the garden

---

[192] Ibid.

[193] *CF* 70.

so well that it took him all afternoon to find them and dig them up. One farmer ended up holding only his pig's tail after the soldiers cut it off so they could take the animal.

As for Louis, it took all the affection he had for his family to keep him from engaging in the counteroffensive. This brave and patriotic military son chose self-denial, but he took the risk anyway to do surveillance on the enemy's advance, which could have cost him his life. When the Prussians arrived in Le Mans in December, the Martin parents were worried about Pauline and Marie who were at the Visitation Monastery at that time. Zélie decided to make the trip to bring them back and arrived in a region ravaged by war: "We see only sadness and devastation; my heart is broken"; thinking of the situation of her family and her country, she added, "We have never been more unfortunate."[194]

At the beginning of January the Prussians entered Alençon. "I cannot describe our anxieties to you," Zélie wrote.[195] Bombs preceded their entrance, so the whole family took refuge in the cellar. Shells were falling all over Rue Pont-Neuf, but the family home was spared. The battle was short but bloody. Zélie saw soldiers returning disfigured and maimed, and she commented with her typical common sense, "Is it reasonable when we have so few men to send them out against an army of enemies like the one we see and then have them butchered?"[196]

In fact, 25,000 Prussians had entered the city with impressive war gear. At the sight of their black flags and the skulls on their helmets, the Martins trembled with fear. The Prussians assigned nine soldiers to be housed with them, but Zélie didn't get upset: "I am not shy with them. When they ask for too much, I tell them it is impossible."[197]

---

[194] *CF* 63.
[195] *CF* 64.
[196] Ibid.
[197] *CF* 63.

As for Louis, he was devastated, grieved not only for the crushing defeat of his country, but also for the desolation that followed. One part of the region was in ruins, there was a shortage of food, and the sick and wounded numbered in the thousands. Louis was so distressed that for several days he could neither eat nor sleep. Zélie was his support and reassured him. Through all this we catch a glimpse of the bright force of this woman whom so many sorrows had failed to crush. She took the reins of the family—"Everybody is crying except me"[198]—with the firm confidence of someone who was not attached to the things of this world: "So, what can we do? When this turmoil is over, we will pick up the pieces that remain, and we will manage to find a way to live with less."[199]

The Martins' patriotism was combined with a sense of humanity that excluded all partisan hatred. Noticing the sadness of one of the soldiers she was lodging, Zélie gave him some sweets and took the time to talk to him. Louis asked mercy for another soldier who was caught stealing from his jewelry store, an offense punishable by death.

A sign from heaven revived their confidence in the future of the country. Zélie read in the newspaper that on January 17, 1871, the Blessed Virgin appeared in Pontmain; as a result of this good news she considered France saved at that point. Ten days later, in fact, the armistice was signed and the Germans gradually left France. For Rue du Pont-Neuf, the war had left its toll: houses listed as uninhabitable, unrecoverable debts, commerce momentarily suspended. Although the Martins were quickly able to get back on their feet, Louis ever after suffered from the fact that his cherished city of Strasbourg was lost in the war to annexation by Prussia.

In the aftermath of all these trials, the arrival of Thérèse, "the greatest saint of modern times," was announced. She would be

---

[198] *CF* 64.

[199] *CF* 66.

described as "a masterpiece of nature and of grace"—and a masterpiece of her parents, we could add. From the first mention of her presence in the womb, Zélie was overjoyed and looked forward to this new little baby: "I hope that this child does well; misfortune does not always come to the same door. In any case, may God's will be done!"[200] The least that can be said of Zélie's comment is that it did describe the child.

During her pregnancy with Thérèse, Zélie had nightmares almost every night, fearing that she could lose her. But as always, it was also a time of special joy for the mother who recounted an episode worthy of the *Golden Legend*.[201] "While I was carrying her," she wrote, "I noticed one thing that never happened with any of my other children. When I would sing, she would sing with me. . . . I confide this to you, because no one would believe it."[202]

Thérèse was born on January 2, 1873, and soon justified her mother's fears. Traumatized by the earlier unfair death of their first Thérèse, Louis and Zélie tried to keep the baby with them, feeding her from drinking cups. But when Thérèse fell ill, Zélie ran in despair to Sémallé to find Rose Taillé. The two women traveled the five miles to Rue Saint-Blaise as fast as they could where they found Thérèse dying:

> I went up to my room, I knelt at the feet of St. Joseph, and I asked him for the grace of healing for the little one, while resigning myself to God's will. I do not often cry, but I was crying as I prayed. I didn't know if I should go downstairs. . . . In the end, I decided to go down, and what did I see? The baby was nursing vigorously. She did not let go until 1:00 p.m.; she spit up a bit and fell back as though dead on her wet nurse.

---

[200] *CF* 80.

[201] A popular thirteenth-century compilation of saints' lives.

[202] *CF* 85.

There were five of us around her. Everyone was stunned. There was a worker who was crying; I felt my blood run cold. The baby had no visible breath. It did no good for us to lean over to try to discover a sign of life because we could see nothing. But she was so calm, so peaceful, that I thanked God for having her die so gently. Then a quarter of an hour went by, and my little Thérèse opened her eyes and started to smile.[203]

Thérèse was rescued but had to go live with Rose Taillé for a year. This time the cruel separation was compensated for by knowing their child was in good health and in good hands.

That same year, 1873, illness knocked again at the Martin door. This time it was Marie who had come down with typhoid fever. Louis and Zélie were dismayed and took turns at the bedside of the young girl who was delirious with fever. When the sickness was prolonged, Louis left on pilgrimage—a little more than nine miles away, on foot and fasting—to beg for the healing of his eldest daughter. Zélie, with the goal of encouraging her daughter to cling to life, explained to her that she had been counting on her to take care of the home when she would no longer be there. This revelation didn't have the anticipated effect on Marie who, at age thirteen, was now discovering that her mother was not immortal. But Zélie, who knew the fragility of life well, was already charting out the future for her family.

Marie finally started to recover to her parents' great relief. Zélie spent hours outlining to her all that she would be able to do once she was healed, and Louis was so happy that he could refuse her nothing. One night, when she could still hardly stand up, Marie insisted on joining the rest of the family for dinner. "I fought vigorously with her not to do that, but she started crying and Papa

---

[203] *CF* 89.

gave in!"[204] Zélie, following the doctors' recommendations, forbade her from eating anything except bouillon. One can imagine Marie's eyes imploring her Papa . . . and he succumbed: "Her father gave her two mouthfuls of cheese and then this and that."[205]

During the long weeks of Marie's illness, Zélie had not forgotten Pauline who was alone at the Visitation Monastery, separated from her sister for the first time. So when she was watching over Marie day and night, working, taking care of the other children, and, according to her, not even taking time to eat, Zélie flooded her second daughter with mail to keep her current on family happenings. Pauline stayed at the Visitation Monastery during vacation time so as not to risk catching Marie's illness, and her mother did everything she could to console her. She proposed having her make Alençon lace and was ready to teach that skill to her daughter, but only if she would enjoy it! She sent her all the material she would need to work at it, as well as a nice portion of chocolate.

The years that followed didn't bring major trials for the Martins. The postwar boom finally brought them a stable prosperity, just as it had the Guérin family. The business for Louis and Zélie was going better than ever, to their great exhaustion, and Isidore's pharmacy became very profitable. Zélie was relieved to see her brother come out of economic stagnation and to see the Christian activities that he took on during that time. In 1874, he cooperated in founding the St. Vincent de Paul Society and the Catholic Circle in Lisieux and became a member of his parish council. Being a loving sister, Zélie had a higher goal for him: "You are becoming a man of merit, and I'm very happy about that, but I want you above all to become saint."[206] She added,

---

[204] *CF* 101.

[205] Ibid.

[206] *CF* 116.

with humility, "However, before desiring holiness for others, I would do well to follow that road myself, something I'm not doing now, but I hope that in time will come."[207]

Marie came home from boarding school for good during the summer of 1875 and Zélie took advantage of that time to train her on how to run a household and be a gentle mother. Marie, despite her mother's advice, made Thérèse eat more than she should have one day, and it made her sick. Zélie, who spent the night at the child's bedside, merely told her oldest daughter that it was a good lesson. With the enthusiasm of youth, Marie was at times too demanding of her younger siblings. One day she sharply remarked to Céline that if she only did sacrifices she liked, then she should not do any at all. Zélie took the occasion to give her a minor lesson in motherly wisdom: "I told Marie she shouldn't discourage her sister like that. It was not possible for such a young child to become a saint instantly, and she should let little things go."[208]

Patiently, providentially, Zélie formed the one who would replace her. Behind the education that Marie would later give her little sisters in Lisieux, we can recognize Zélie's firm yet gentle hand. For the moment, in any case, Marie was a great help to her mother. Zélie could work quietly while Marie took care of Céline and Thérèse. The overworked mother began to see her burden lightened and hoped for better days when Pauline would return too. "I am building castles in air and dreaming of happiness and peace!"[209] That was Zélie's dream: to enjoy her family finally reunited but—and these were the last words she wrote— "God wants me to rest elsewhere than on the earth."[210]

---

[207] Ibid.
[208] *CF* 172.
[209] *CF* 143.
[210] *CF* 217.

Chapter 8

ZÉLIE'S SUFFERING AND PASSION

In 1865, when she was thirty-four years old, Zélie complained to her brother about a painful gland in her breast. This might have been a cyst, easily diagnosed by doctors today. Louis was worried, and the couple thought for while about an operation, but then it seemed to be forgotten. Eleven years later, in the summer of 1876, Zélie began to suffer again. Isidore gave her some medicine, but it was ineffective. A few months later Zélie decided to see a doctor. This was a week before Christmas. Zélie told the Guérin family:

> I went to Doctor X who, after having thoroughly examined and prodded me, said after a moment of silence, "Do you know that what you have is very serious? It's a fibroid tumor. Would you be closed to having an operation?" I answered, "No, but I'm sure that instead of saving my life this operation would shorten my days." I added some proof to support what I said so well that he responded immediately, "You know as much as I do. All of what you say is true, and I cannot advise you to do it since the outcome is doubtful." I asked him if there was a one in a hundred chance of success, and he answered evasively. I'm grateful to him for his frankness because I will hurry now to set my affairs in order so as not to

leave my family in difficulty. He offered me a prescription. When I asked him, "What good would that do?" he looked at me and replied, "No good at all. I do that to please the patients."

I couldn't stop myself from telling all this to the family. I'm sorry now that I did that because it caused a scene of grief. . . . Everybody was crying, and poor Léonie was sobbing. But I told them how many people had that same condition for ten to fifteen years, and I seemed so calm in saying it cheerfully the way I always did—maybe even more cheerfully—that I calmed everybody down a bit.

I am, however, far from deceiving myself, and I have a hard tine sleeping at night when I think about the future. Nevertheless, I'm resigning myself the best I can, but I was far from expecting such a trial. . . . My husband cannot be comforted. He stopped his fishing excursions, he put up his fishing lines in the attic, and he doesn't go to our circle of friends any more. He's devastated. . . .

I'm not suffering much. There is swelling on one whole side right up to my underarm, a dull pain in the spot where the tumor is. I cannot lie down on that side. I don't want you to worry too much about this and want you to resign yourself to God's will. If he found me very useful on earth, he would certainly not have allowed me to have this sickness, because I prayed to him so much not to take me out of this world as long as I was needed by my children. . . .

It comforts me to know that there are good relatives who could replace us well in case of misfortune. There are some poor mothers much more unfortunate than I who do not know what will happen to their children, who leave them in need, without help from anyone. As for me I have nothing to fear in that regard. In brief, I do not see things darkly, and that is a great grace that God has given me. . . . Whatever happens, let's profit from the good times that remain and let's not worry ourselves. Besides, things will always be what God wants.[211]

Zélie knew the doctor had given up on her, but she still went around talking about it as her "little boo boo,"[212] so as not to worry her relatives. She knew the loneliness of the sick who know that death is at their door while their relatives refuse to accept it. Seeking not so much to be consoled as to console, she sacrificed her last Christmas with the family to go to Lisieux to reassure the Guérin family who were crushed by the news. She wrote to her husband, "After dinner I did everything I could to cheer my brother up and give him a bit of courage."[213] To comfort her husband she added:

Doctor Notta seems to be saying that I can carry on for a long time in my condition, so let us put ourselves back into God's hands. He knows better than we do what we need. "He is the one who wounds and the one who heals" [see Jb 5:18]. I will go to Lourdes on the first pilgrimage, and I hope that the Blessed Mother will heal me, if that is necessary. While we wait, let's be calm. I rejoice to be seeing you all again. The time seems so long! I would have wanted to come back today! I am happy only when I am with you, my dear Louis."[214]

---

[211] *CF* 177.
[212] *CF* 178.
[213] *CF* 179.
[214] Ibid.

All of her maternal and sensitive charity was on display during the time of her last illness. She was quiet with others about her suffering and her worries. She went so far as to hide her illness from her sister, who was also sick, as well as from Pauline, in order to prevent her from stopping her studies at the Visitation Monastery. However, we know how much she wanted Pauline with her. When she spoke or wrote to her, it was to demonstrate her love, to comfort her, to encourage her. Louis supported Zélie as much as he could, but during her last months Zélie leaned especially on the Lord.

A few weeks before knowing she was sick, Zélie had written that she wasn't stronger than anyone else in the face of a trial. "[My sister] thinks that I desire great suffering because I told her that I would prefer to die of a slow illness if I had a choice."[215] Zélie was actually most afraid of dying without being able to prepare for it. "But great suffering, no, I do not have enough virtue to desire that, and I dread that!"[216] She also wrote, "The desire to live is not lacking."[217] But all her life she had abandoned herself to God's will, offering him her suffering, and she would reach the ultimate degree with this gift. The whole family, all the relatives, began to pray to obtain the miracle of her healing. Zélie joked about it: "If I were the Blessed Virgin, I would yield very quickly to so many prayers just to get rid of all these people."[218]

Isidore loaded her up with medicine and medical advice that was more or less applicable, while Louis urged her to make pilgrimages. Zélie pictured the future of her children in her absence and gently prepared them for the inevitable: "I rely in fact only

---

[215] *CF* 173.
[216] Ibid.
[217] *CF* 186.
[218] *CF* 187.

on the help of our good Mother! If she wants to, she could in fact heal me, since she has healed much sicker people. I am not convinced, however, that she will heal me because that could very well not be God's will."[219]

Zélie had a presentiment about her approaching death. She could have, understandably rebelled however, when she wrote, "Must I see the dream of my whole life [to have her family together and thriving] evaporate right at the moment that it was to become reality?"[220] In fact, Pauline was getting ready to finish her schooling in Le Mans and the whole family was finally about to be reunited. But, completely abandoned to God, she experienced tremendous peace:

> God is in fact giving me the grace not to be afraid. I am very calm, and I find myself almost happy. I would not change my lot for anything. If God wants to heal me I would be very happy because deep down I want to live. It is costing me something to leave my husband and my children. But on the other hand, I say to myself, "If I am not healed, it is because it would be perhaps more useful for them if I went away. . . ." While I wait, I will do all I can to get a miracle; I am counting on the pilgrimage to Lourdes. But if I am not healed I will try to sing on my way home anyway.[221]

We might be surprised that she wasn't more anxious about the future of her family, but the attitude of this deeply believing woman reflected Christ's words when he left his apostles so he could send them his Spirit: "It is to your advantage that I go

---

[219] *CF* 181.
[220] *CF* 212.
[221] *CF* 189.

away" (Jn 16:7). She believed wholeheartedly that God could take better care of her family than she could.

Her faith also relied on knowing her daughters' hearts. Her two eldest were practically adults who were capable of raising the younger ones, whom she was pleased to see were already growing up in a good way. Unaware of how prophetic she was being, she wrote about Thérèse, "I assure you that this one will turn out well."[222] As for Léonie, Zélie didn't believe she could help her as long as the child was opposing her. She knew that she could count on her husband to take care of all these little ones.

In order to relieve everyone's worry, Zélie behaved as though nothing was wrong, and she did it so well that she maintained family life almost to the very end the way it had been before she became ill. Life went on with the minor illnesses of the children, orders of Alençon lace to fulfill, a retreat at the parish, and so on. Zélie, a bit weary of her brother's prodding—he still wanted her to have an operation and asked her to go back to the doctor, and even to consult someone in Paris—finally wrote: "Look, let's please stop talking about my illness anymore. It's starting to get boring. Let's leave it aside and talk about happier things."[223]

In perfectly applying her own instructions, Zélie wrote letters at the beginning of 1877 that are even livelier than her earlier ones. She recounted how Léonie had inadvertently prepared soup for the whole family . . . kitchen dishtowel soup![224] Or how she discovered that Thérèse, who was very good at the "*chapelet de practiques*,"[225] added a bead for a silly remark she made to Cé-

---

[222] *CF* 212.

[223] *CF* 186.

[224] See *CF185* for the incident.

[225] This was a rosary of thirty beads; every sacrifice or invocation would mean the advance of one bead; any sin or "bad thought" would mean the regression of one bead.

line. Her mother commented that given what she had said it was better to go back one bead, and little Thérèse replied, "Oh! Well, I don't know where my chaplet is right now."[226]

Zélie's principle correspondence was with Sister Marie-Dosithée who, after years of illness, finally died at the Visitation Monastery. This wasn't a small trial for Zélie, but Sister Marie-Dosithée, despite her suffering, was overjoyed at the approach of death, and she prepared for it as though it were a great feast. Like Teresa of Ávila, she could have exclaimed, "I want to see God!" Her example deeply impressed Zélie who was preparing to travel down a similar path. "I never saw anything so edifying,"[227] she wrote after seeing her joyful, peaceful sister for one of the last times.

Sister Marie-Dosithée faded slowly on February 24. Zélie received a letter from the Visitation sisters that she didn't have the courage to open. Louis gently took the letter and read it to his wife:

> It was this morning at 7:00 a.m. that our very dear Sister Marie-Dosithée came to the end of her edifying life with a death worthy of envy. For two days, a notable weakening let us know that the end was approaching. Difficulty breathing and a kind of ongoing distress made our dear sick sister suffer more, although she did not lose her peace or her perfect resignation and felt more and more the desire to go see Our Lord. . . . We can say, dear Madame, that you and we have another holy protector in heaven . . . because it would be difficult to end a very virtuous life in a more saintly way. . . . Oh! How she will be praying for the two dear families that she loved so much.[228]

---

[226] *CF* 192.

[227] *CF* 167.

[228] Quoted in *CF* 190.

Sister Marie-Dosithée died with the "odor of sanctity," as we say. At the convent and in the city everyone said, "The saint is dead," and many came to see her mortal remains in the chancel before her burial. "When they carried her out to the cemetery, there was no impression of sadness; it seemed instead to be a triumph. The sisters said they had never experienced that before."[229]

Zélie had written many years earlier, "I will lose everything if I lose her."[230] But if the separation was undoubtedly terribly painful, Zélie was comforted in knowing that her sister was not suffering any more and, above all, that she had attained her joyful goal. "This is all very sad, but we will always have the consolation of knowing her to be in heaven, and for me that is the essential thing."[231]

Besides, Zélie had entrusted to her sister before her death some "commissions" for heaven, in which we see Zélie speaking to the saints with the same humorous familiarity that she did with her relatives: "As soon as you get to paradise, go find the Blessed Virgin and tell her, 'My good Mother, you played a trick on my sister in giving her poor Léonie; she was not like the child we had asked you for. You need to fix the situation.' After that, go find Blessed Margaret-Mary and tell her, 'Why did you heal her [Léonie] miraculously? It would have been better to let her die because you are supposed to rectify misfortunes.' [My sister] scolded me for talking like that, but I did not have bad intentions, as God well knows."[232]

Léonie, who was thirteen years old and entering a difficult adolescence was still Zélie's greatest concern: "It is her future

---

[229] *CF* 197.

[230] *CF* 43.

[231] *CF* 176.

[232] *CF* 182.

that worries me the most."[233] Zélie soon after said: "The poor child has loads of faults. We just don't know how to handle her. But God is so merciful that I have always had hope and I still have hope."[234]

One small detail had kindled this hope. Before the death of her aunt, Léonie absolutely insisted on writing her a letter whose contents made her mother incredulous and amazed: "My dear Aunt, I always keep the picture you gave me as a relic. I look at it every day like you told me to, to become obedient. Marie had it framed for me. My dear Aunt, when you are in heaven, please ask God if he would give me the grace to be converted and also give me the vocation to become a real religious because I think of it every day."[235]

Zélie commented: "What do you say to that? I am quite surprised. Where did she get those ideas? I am certainly not the one who put them in her head. I am very convinced that unless there is a miracle, my Léonie could never be part of a community."[236] When the astonished family asked her why she insisted on asking to be a "real" religious, she answered, "It means that I want to be a religious who is completely good and in the end to be a saint."[237] So those were the commissions entrusted to Sister Marie-Dosithée who undoubtedly discharged them without delay.

At the beginning of March 1877, in fact, Marie went by the kitchen and was shocked to hear the maid, Louise Marais, who had been working for the family for eleven years, threaten Léonie violently. The Martins made the horrifying discovery that for a long time the maid had been mistreating Léonie under the

---

[233] *CF* 184.
[234] *CF* 185.
[235] Ibid.
[236] Ibid.
[237] Ibid.

family roof. Threatened with beatings, the poor child had to do the maid's work and obey her in all things, and obey only her. Louise had used all the subterfuges possible to conceal the tyranny she was exercising over the child and promised to deliver an unforgettable correction if Léonie ever complained.

Zélie later said that she would have quite simply been incapable of guessing what was going on: "I would never have believed that someone could go so far and do such cold things as she has."[238] In addition to the hell she was living in because of the maid, Léonie had a more or less conscious grudge against her parents who were oblivious to the situation and were not defending her. So when Léonie saw her parents energetically rush to her assistance (and their anger against Louise was in proportion to their horror over the situation), Léonie totally changed her attitude toward them and in particular toward her mother. With trust reestablished between them, Léonie was always at Zélie's side, and she did all she could to please her mother. She became joyful and obedient and began to blossom. Her mother was shocked by all this and devoted herself completely to this child for whom she had hoped for so long. "She loves me as much as it is possible to love," she stated with emotion, "and with that love, God's love is penetrating her own heart bit by bit."[239] For Zélie all of this was the result of her sister's prayers in heaven.

Zélie felt a sense of urgency, fearful that her sickness would take her away from Léonie too early. She had peacefully accepted the idea of dying, convinced that she was no longer indispensable to her daughters, but she now underwent a massive change, seized by a strong desire to live, not for herself but for Léonie and the help she could give her. Afraid that her daughter's new equilibrium would be damaged by her death, she wanted to

---

[238] *CF* 195.
[239] *CF* 200.

satisfy her maternal thirst to see Léonie find herself at last. Zélie started then to pray in earnest and with great hope for her own healing. She wrote to her sister-in-law, "The sicker I am, the more hope I will have," and added with faith, "I will not die for a long time."[240]

As for the maid, Louis and Zélie treated her justly. Shocked, at first they immediately fired her. Louise groaned and wept in vain, since Zélie couldn't even stand to look at her. Quite quickly, however, they asked themselves if they had done the right thing. Didn't forgiving mean bringing justice and mercy to people and offering them a second chance? Justice had to be done for Louise: completely devoted to the Martins for years, she was entirely loyal to Zélie and had really thought she was helping her, as surprising as that sounds, in roughly treating Léonie's difficult character. So, despite their anger, Louis and Zélie took her in again and decided to get counsel about the best way to handle things. Zélie went to her beloved Poor Clare sisters and consulted an elderly sister who had the reputation of being a saint. The sister recommended waiting and not doing anything hastily.

The Martins finally reached a compromise: Louise could stay in service to the family until Zélie died but was forbidden to talk to Léonie. She had to leave the young girl alone so as to avoid any risk of taking control over her again. It was hard for Zélie, though, to continue seeing the woman whose actions she couldn't forget, so she solicitously watched over Léonie.

Louise took care of her mistress with faultless devotion and would later find another job without difficulty. She testified right to the end of her life about the goodness of the Martins.

As the weeks went on, Zélie could feel the illness spreading. From February 1877 on, swollen glands, which indicated the cancer's metastasis, appeared on her neck. She redoubled her

---

[240] *CF* 193.

prayer and decided with Louis to set an ending date to their lace business, cherishing the hope that she would then live only for her family and in particular be able to devote to Léonie all the time she needed.

The honesty of the Martins was again demonstrated in the sale of their business: "The deal with Alençon lace is not over. . . . Moreover, I prayed to the Sacred Heart for the sale not to go through if it would be a bad investment for the people who want to buy it. Had we wanted, the sale could have easily been done. But I thought I needed to open the eyes of the buyers to certain difficulties because they were rosy-eyed about it, and I was not happy about that."[241] Providence always responds to such righteousness. During the delay, Louis and Zélie discovered that they were dealing with swindlers! As so often happened at the beginning of the year, the orders for lace dropped on their own, making Zélie believe once again that her business was drying up. They abandoned the idea of selling just then. Zélie ended up working right up until her death, even though it was at a less intense pace than in the past.

A few weeks later, Zélie heard about a pilgrimage to Lourdes. The family decided that she would go with Marie, Pauline, and Léonie from June 18 to 22 along with people from the Diocese of Angers. The clearly defined goal: to obtain a miracle for Zélie from the Blessed Virgin.

The Martins' approach to requesting a miracle is instructive. First of all, a miracle is not deserved. Zélie was at first a bit embarrassed about asking God for a departure from the laws of nature for herself, but, "What is certain is that he often does that out of sheer goodness and mercy."[242] Her brother noted that God could do this miracle solely for his own glory, which earned him

---

[241] *CF* 183.
[242] *CF* 202.

a response that showed the heights Zélie had reached: "I too say that everything is for the glory of God, but he does not generally think about himself; we need a miracle for me, even if no one in the world would know about it."[243] It is the summit of holiness to recognize the passionate love of the Father for his children, a summit that her daughter Thérèse would also reach.

Next, in faith they would mobilize the Communion of Saints to solicit the miracle: novenas, Masses, and prayers by the whole family, in particular the children and friends at the convent. Zélie was very touched by this support but also invoked the Church in heaven: "No, never has heaven ever seen or ever will see such fervent prayers and such lively faith. And then I have a sister in heaven who cares for me, and I also have my four little angels who will pray for me; they will all be at Lourdes with us."[244]

In other respects, as always, the will of God was predominant. Zélie didn't pretend to know better than God and warned her daughters before leaving for Lourdes, "We need to dispose ourselves to accept the will of the good Lord with open hearts, whatever it is, because his will is always what is best for us."[245]

Finally, Zélie was unable to be concerned about only herself. What she was asking at Lourdes was, of course, her own healing, but she was also asking for healing for Pauline, who had worrisome headaches, and above all healing for Léonie's heart: "I will entreat [the Blessed Virgin] to heal my child, to open up her understanding, and to make her a saint."[246] From the beginning Zélie was aware that she wasn't making this pilgrimage only for herself, and that certainty increased during the long journey.

---

[243] *CF* 205.
[244] Ibid.
[245] *CF* 204.
[246] *CF* 206.

The Martins' lesson of intercession is this: a humble and confident request is openhearted and completely surrendered in terms of the answer. The answer would not be Zélie's healing, but, as we will see, the answer would be in line with the confidence of the seekers.

Zélie, Léonie, Marie, and Pauline left for Lourdes full of faith. Zélie didn't like taking trips but, as she put it so well, it was a question this time of "running after life."[247] But it was to life that the Lord was calling her. The lives of God's close friends often entail a way of the cross in death and the moments that precede it. Reflecting the pattern of Christ, these people seem to go beyond human limitations, expressing a heroic faith in proportion to the happiness they will experience in heaven. This is the case for martyrs, and was so for Thérèse and her parents as well.

The last stage of Zélie's life began with the pilgrimage to Lourdes, which turned out to be especially difficult. The children were sick—"Despite the affectionate protestations of my daughters to take care of me, I in fact was the one [who] was taking care of them"[248]—and Zélie never succeeded in sleeping on the train because some travelers spilled coffee accidentally all over the girls' things. When they got set up at the hotel where the exhausted girls unpacked, Zélie and Pauline discovered they had lost the rosaries that were souvenirs from the aunt in Le Mans. They even participated in the burial of a pilgrim who had died from having drunk too much water at Lourdes!

Zélie was not used to swimming pools, so immersing herself in a pool of water at Lourdes was difficult: "I looked with terror at that icy water and that deathly cold marble. But I had to cooperate, so I jumped in courageously. Yes, but . . . I almost choked,

---

[247] *CF* 207.
[248] *CF* 209.

and I had to get out almost immediately."[249] They quickly used up the water bottles of Lourdes, one after another, and Zélie fell down carrying one; she wasn't able to see the priest she had wanted to meet; and she missed her return train. But the biggest disappointment was that she wasn't healed.

The fatigue and the mishaps of the journey had, on the contrary, aggravated her illness. The girls were in despair and Louis had spent a horrible week "hoping every minute for the awaited telegram [announcing the miracle], and every time the doorbell rang he got nervous."[250] Upon their return, they had to face the smirks of their nonbelieving neighbors who had been mocking the path the Martins were taking. In brief, the whole family had plenty to be discouraged about. It can be a harsh blow to put one's trust in God when a miracle, sought with all one's strength, doesn't happen. But this was Zélie's reaction instead: "Tell me, could we have had a worse trip? Of course there are great graces hidden beneath all this that will compensate for all the troubles. By faith, I put miraculous water on my Léonie's forehead."[251]

The association of ideas here is revealing. Clearly seeing that the trip didn't turn out the way everyone had hoped, Zélie reoriented her prayer, offering everything for Léonie's sake. Zélie added heroic charity to her act of faith in the face of an apparent failure: Now that she was worn out, it was she who sustained the whole family. "[Louis] was surprised to see me come back so happily as though I had obtained the desired grace; that gave him courage and brought a good mood back into the house."[252] She was reassuring to her family, exhorting each family member

---

[249] Ibid.
[250] *CF* 210.
[251] *CF* 209.
[252] *CF* 210.

to have courage and faith, and calming their worries by her radiating peace.

Her peace was undoubtedly the first fruit of her pilgrimage to Lourdes. In light of later facts, everyone's fervent prayers had not been in vain, and in hindsight we can perceive signs of God's response, even if the unanswered prayer for healing bears the seal of the secrets of the King. Another fruit of Lourdes was that Zélie seemed to understand that the Blessed Virgin would favorably replace her in terms of her daughters. At her return, she wrote Pauline to comfort her: "Pray with faith to the Mother of Mercies. She will come to our assistance with the goodness and the gentleness of the most affectionate mother."[253]

All the Martin daughters experienced the motherhood of Mary in a significant way. The most obvious example was the day Mary, from her statue at Thérèse's bedside, smiled at her, freeing her from a serious illness and from the sorrow at the loss of her mother. And she accompanied Zélie during her last weeks in a special way, as described by Zélie: "Fortunately the Blessed Virgin helped me; otherwise I don't know what would have become of me."[254]

Léonie would be the last visible fruit of this pilgrimage, but more broadly the fruit of Zélie's efforts, prayers, and offerings. Léonie was in some way Zélie's masterpiece. She would become a holy religious and, after Thérèse, the most beloved and the most prayed to Martin daughter, touching hearts because of her own difficulties. The death of her mother didn't throw her into darkness, just the opposite. There is no doubt that she owed her graces to Zélie's confidence that went beyond human wisdom in entrusting her child to God, counting on him to have a better influence on her than her mother's heart could have had if she had lived.

---

[253] Ibid.
[254] *CF* 212.

Some days after her trip to Lourdes, Zélie was still hoping for a miracle, but, based on the evidence, she quickly became aware of the progress of her illness. She was going to die, and it was time to prepare for the grand encounter that she had hoped for all her life.

At the beginning of July 1877 the first attack occurred. Her final letters leave us horrible evidence of her sufferings. In that era, doctors were unable to alleviate great pain. On the night of July 7, when Louis was at Nocturnal Adoration and Zélie was alone, she had horrendous pain in her neck, which made her feel that her head was going to come off. This didn't prevent her, though, from getting up the next morning to go to Mass, where she had to hold back from crying out in pain. Some people would say this was a lack of prudence, but it was actually a question of priorities: Facing death, Zélie easily made the choice between momentary relief from pain and the Eucharist. As long as she could drag herself there, she continued going to Mass with the help of Louis and Marie until the end of August, at the cost of unbearable suffering. Marie recounted: "Friday she went to the 7:00 Mass because it was the First Friday of the month. Papa took her because she would not have been able to go without him. She told us that on arriving at the church, she never would have been able to go in if someone had not been there to help open the doors."[255]

Her pain didn't make her withdraw. In that month of July she said a novena for one of her workers who was sick, she continued to send humorous and reassuring letters, she kept herself back from calling anyone or crying out at night so as not to wake anyone, and she kept a good atmosphere in the house. But her illness was rapidly progressing. "I cannot dress or undress myself alone," she wrote on July 15.

---

[255] *LT*, Letter from Marie Martin to Céline Guérin, August 9, 1877.

My arm is limp on the side where the tumor is, but my hand still wants to hold a needle! In addition, I have been experiencing a general malaise, intestinal pain, and fever for about fifteen days. Finally, I cannot remain standing and I need to sit down. . . . I have almost no attacks during the day, but at night when my ligaments become stiff I need to take unheard of precautions to change position. Meanwhile, I have learned how the process works, and I am beginning to know what to do to get relief and avoid an attack.[256]

She offered all of these sufferings for her relatives and was preparing for heaven, as she wrote to Pauline humorously: "You say that you would like to suffer for me. I would be quite annoyed at that. You must not want me to gain heaven, and you must want everything for yourself. . . . Well, feel free, my Pauline! As for me, I would probably have to spend one hundred years in Purgatory! Would you like to do those years for me too? When it comes to it, why not take it all?"[257] The only thing she was asking from those around her from then on was that they pray for her to abandon herself totally to God's will and to accept pain with peace and patience.

Learning of the worsening of her condition, Isidore came to visit at the beginning of August. Because of his pharmaceutical knowledge, Zélie had earlier asked him to warn her if he foresaw death approaching. Without any tact or circumspection and in front of a crushed Louis, he announced to his sister that she had less than one month to live. Zélie didn't flinch and responded that she didn't fear death. When she was alone with him, she wondered what was going to happen to poor Louis and her five

---

[256] *CF* 213.
[257] *CF* 214.

daughters, but as always, she put them in God's hands. Isidore proposed that she urge her husband to move to Lisieux after her death so that the Guérin family could help him. Touched by that proposal, Zélie felt it would be the best solution. She talked to Louis about it but respected him too much to force his hand, something that would have been easy for her to do in that situation.

During the month of August, the pain increased to unbearable levels. Zélie had a last respite on August 9, and she took advantage of that to attend a little festivity her daughters had prepared for handing out prizes from "the Visitation Sainte Marie of Alençon," a grand name given by Marie to the short courses she had been giving Céline and Thérèse. Louis and Zélie presided at the ceremony in a very serious way in Marie's room, which had been completely redecorated for the occasion, giving out prizes and crowns to the little winners. Marie even gave a speech.

In the following weeks, Zélie cried because she couldn't give her daughters any distraction, so she urged Louis to plan a boat outing, which was surely not the happiest. Suffering completely took over:

> My dear brother, I was crying out to you loudly yesterday, believing that you alone could bring me relief. I suffered for twenty-four hours more than I ever suffered during my whole life, so those hours were spent groaning and crying. . . . I was in a horribly awkward position and unable to lay my head anywhere. People tried everything, but my poor head could touch nothing, and I could not make the least movement even to swallow liquid. My neck was stiff on all sides and to move it even the slightest bit brought terrible pain. Finally I was able to stay in bed as long as I was in a sitting position. When

sleep tried to come, the minimal movement that I had made was doubtless what awakened all the pain again. I moaned all night. Louis, Marie, and the maid stayed close to me. Poor Louis, at times he would take me in his arms like a child.[258]

In the midst of her suffering Zélie turned toward heaven. Marie would hear her groan during her insomnia, "O you, who created me, have mercy on me!" and another time she found her on her knees, ghastly pale, saying her Rosary before the statue of the Blessed Virgin. Like Christ and many of his saints, Zélie felt herself abandoned by heaven at times: "I was imploring all the saints in heaven, one after another, but no one answered me."[259] None of this prevented her from having a profound serenity admired by people such as her confessor who was much less calm than she was, according to Louis. She often repeated the saying of St. Francis de Sales, "One ounce of virtue practiced in tribulation is worth more than a thousand in a time of rest and joy," and put it into practice.

Between two fierce attacks of intense pain, she had her daughters come so she could give them her final advice, inviting them to holiness and entrusting the younger ones to the older ones. Above all she told them again and again that she loved them. Louis, brokenhearted, didn't leave her bedside.

On August 25, Zélie had a hemorrhage that drained her last bit of strength. On August 26, Louis went to find a priest to give her last rites, which she received surrounded by her whole family in prayer. Louis could not hold back his sobs. From that moment on Zélie suffered less, and although conscious she could neither move nor speak. But her eyes still spoke. When Isidore

---

[258] *CF* 216.
[259] Ibid.

and his wife arrived on August 27, Zélie looked at Céline Guérin for a long time and smiled at her. Céline would later write to the Martin girls: "I thought I understood her gaze, which nothing could ever make me forget; it is engraved on my heart. Since that day, I have tried to replace the one whom God took from you."[260] Thérèse would write concerning her mother,

> I liked Maman's smile.
> Her profound glance seemed to say,
> "Eternity is ravishing me and drawing me . . .
> I am going up to a blue heaven
> To see God."[261]

At half past midnight on August 28 Zélie slipped away gently with Louis and Isidore at her side. Her last written words were: "If the Blessed Virgin does not heal me, it is because my time is over and God wants me to rest somewhere else besides the earth."[262] After a life of labor, joy, and suffering, the one who was completely devoted to God and her family reached her port and was reunited with her four angels she had grieved over so much. Learning of her death, her confessor said that there was one more saint in heaven.

The family gathered around her body at the church. "She seemed to be sleeping," writes Father Piat. "Having almost reached the age of forty-six, one would have said she was taken away much too soon. Her emaciated face, sculpted by suffering, had taken on a striking expression of majesty and youth during her passing. An impressive atmosphere of welcome and supernatural calm enveloped the chapel. Mr. Martin and his daughters

---

[260] *LT*, Letter of Céline Guérin to Thérèse, November 16, 1891.
[261] *PN* 18, stanza 8.
[262] *CF* 217.

could not stop contemplating the relaxed face of the one who, after having worked so hard, finally knew rest."[263]

She was buried on August 29 in the cemetery of Notre-Dame of Alençon. The terrible death of this mother of five children can be understood in the light of the Gospel: "Unless a grain of wheat falls into the earth and dies, it remains alone; but if it dies, it bears much fruit" (Jn 12:24)—fruit of grace for her family and for so many others that Zélie Martin would help. It is probable that Zélie is not resting much at all up in heaven.

---

[263] *HF*, p. 191.

Chapter 9

LOUIS'S OFFERINGS

After Zélie's death, the Guérins insisted to Louis that he should carry out his wife's last plan and move to Lisieux to be next to them. Isidore and his wife could support him in the education of the girls and, with their own children, Jeanne and Marie, become one big family. Louis soon acquiesced for the good of his children. It was a considerable sacrifice for him, however: His mother, his friends, the Pavilion, his gravesites, and his memories were all in Alençon. Marie commented on it in a letter to her uncle: "He would make all possible sacrifices for us. He would sacrifice his happiness, and even his life if necessary, to make us happy. He backs away from nothing. He does not hesitate for a minute and believes it is his duty and good for everybody, and that is enough for him."[264]

Isidore didn't spare himself either, visiting no fewer than twenty-five houses to find the Martins a place for an ideal life. He found it on September 10, 1887, 764 steps away from his own pharmacy (he counted!)—a lovely home the Martin girls would name "*Les Buissonnnets*."[265] This beautiful, little, middle-class home had a large garden and would be a "soft nest" for the grieving family.

---

[264] Letter quoted in *HF*, p. 196.
[265] "The little bushes."

The daughters, after a goodbye visit to the Notre-Dame cemetery where Zélie was laid to rest, moved in on November 15 with help from the Guérins while Louis stayed behind in Alençon for a few weeks to liquidate the business. He wrote to them from there with some advice: "I clasp all of you close to my heart since I love you, and I entrust you to your holy mother."[266] It was once again a solid hope that supported the family in their trial of grief. They all knew that Zélie was close to them and watching over them, but everyone of course missed her terribly. Louis had not liked being separated from his wife for even just a few days. We can imagine his suffering, then, at being separated from her by death.

The wound for the children was not any less. As Zélie had foreseen, however, her household quickly found its balance: Léonie and Céline chose Marie as a substitute "Maman" while Thérèse turned to Pauline. Marie, who was almost eighteen, valiantly took on the role of mistress of the house and educator of the youngest ones, following her mother's example in promoting the Visitation teaching methods in which she herself had been trained. They organized a new life at *Les Buissonnets*. Louis, according to the title his daughters gave him, was their "beloved king."

Still grieving, the Martins closed ranks and preferred to be with one another and keep to themselves. Louis's attraction to solitude grew with the loss of his wife. He didn't try to enter the social life of Lisieux and was content to visit Alençon every three months or so to see his friends and his mother, who was spending a happy old age with the former wet nurse Rose Taillé, and to pray at the gravesides of his dearly departed. His daughters no longer had any attraction to social events to the point that

---

[266] *CF* 218.

the Martin family spent little time with anyone else except the Guérin family.

They were not relying on themselves, however, but on God. Everyone went to daily Mass, and Louis presided over family prayer at meals and at night. Thérèse wrote that she "only [had] to look at him to see how the saints pray."[267] At times this holy, contemplative man was so inundated by grace that he couldn't hold back tears. Although he left Marie the task of teaching the catechism to the little ones, his attitude was often an occasion of edification for the girls. Seeing God's goodness in all things, he communicated his wonder and God's grace to those around him. Thérèse would later remind her sisters of the things he often repeated, like, "No one can outdo the good Lord for generosity," and "Lord, increase our faith."

As a replacement for the Pavilion, Louis set up the highest room in the house, the belvedere, as a quasi-cell for prayer and study. He spent long hours there praying or reading. No doubt he would join his dear wife in prayer. Something he shared in 1885 demonstrates the strength of this relationship that lasted beyond death: "The thought of your mother follows me constantly."[268]

Louis and Marie both asked Zélie for help in the children's education. Marie was aware that she couldn't replace such a mother and humbly said that she hoped more from the protection of her holy Maman than from her feeble efforts. It was a prayer that brought fruit, in particular with Léonie, about whom she wrote to her father: "I have been noticing that she is changing from day to day for some time now. Haven't you noticed it, my little Father? My uncle and aunt already see it. I am sure that it is our dear mother who is obtaining this grace,

---

[267] Thérèse of Lisieux, *The Story of a Soul* (Washington, DC: ICS Publications, 1996), p. 43.

[268] *CF* 228.

and I am persuaded that our Léonie will be a consolation to us one day."[269]

As for Louis, he added a maternal gentleness to his paternal authority. According to Céline, his heart was exceptionally tender toward his daughters, and he lived only for them: "No mother's heart could have surpassed his, and without any weakness too."[270] The domestic affairs were in Marie's hands, but it was Louis who set the tone and general direction for the family. His values had not changed since Alençon; the house had to be kept up well but always in a spirit of frugality. They lived and ate simply. Louis never tolerated waste or unneeded expense, but he made sure his daughters had all that they needed to blossom: toys, books, pets, and art materials for Pauline and Céline, the artists in the family. However, he opposed all whims, and idleness was forbidden. For him the education of the girls, the management of their affairs, as well as the upkeep of the garden, the aviary, and the farmyard were the center of their activities, along with works of charity, of course.

Among other things, he was involved in the Society of St. Vincent de Paul. He helped a neighboring convent manage their finances, and he spent part of Mondays welcoming the poor into his home. Painting, sewing, the upkeep of the house, and study set the rhythm for his daughters' days. Not being able to separate himself yet from Léonie, Céline, and Thérèse, Louis didn't send them away to boarding school but enrolled them as day students at the Benedictine Abbey of Notre-Dame du Pré, a good school in Lisieux. He often went to pick them up himself and listened to their reports of the day. He taught them to respect the authority of their teachers and of the new servant, Victoire. The servant said the *Les Buissonnets* home was a real

---

[269] Letter quoted in *HF*, p. 297.
[270] See Céline's testimony at the beatification process for Thérèse.

little convent—as much because of the tremendous faith and love that reigned there as because of the home's atmosphere of a cloister.

It was a very joyful home for these dynamic five daughters and their father. Thérèse has left long accounts of their evenings and their Sundays. Every evening, Louis would turn himself into a pastor-emcee for his daughters' entertainment. He would begin by reading and commenting on a spiritual passage, often from *The Liturgical Year*, by Dom Guéranger. And then in his beautiful voice he would sing something from his large repertoire or do funny imitations. Thérèse would be at his knees, drinking it all in, and would make good use of that heritage later at Carmel. Then, when it was time for games, Louis proved himself to be an almost unbeatable checker's player. Finally, they would gather around the statue of Mary to thank her for the day. On Sunday, after the service, they took their traditional walk while Louis shared his knowledge of nature with his daughters, or he would fish while the girls entertained themselves.

The feast day of St. Louis, the king of France, was a day of celebration at *Les Buissonnets*. The girls decorated the house with flowers and garlands, and the five of them would tiptoe upstairs to surprise their father in the belvedere. Thérèse would bring her little poem of congratulations, one of which has been preserved, revealing the love the Martin children had for their "king":

> In growing up I see your soul
> Full of God and love.
> This blessed example inspires me,
> And I want to follow you.
>
> I want to become on earth
> Your joy, your consolation.

I want to imitate you, little Father,
You who are so tender, so sweet, so good.[271]

And then a celebration would follow.

Louis wanted his daughters to know the world. He took them by turns to Paris, to the seashore at Deauville and Trouville where they spent nice vacations with the Guérin family, to the Great Exposition of Le Havre, and so forth. For a time the family lived in the peaceful happiness that Zélie had always wanted for them.

Even if Louis, like his wife, gave complete freedom to his daughters in regard to their own futures, the family atmosphere favored the blossoming of religious vocations. One after another, the Martin daughters would hear a call resonating in their hearts to consecrate themselves. Louis supported each of them in this step, though it was painful for him. Pauline was the first to want to leave the nest, as Zélie had foreseen.

The example of Pauline's Visitation aunt had deeply affected her, but considering the family situation after the death of her mother, Pauline chose to stay home for a while and to support Marie in educating Céline and Thérèse. Her calling became more and more pressing, however, and at the end of 1881, when she was twenty years old, she contacted the Visitation Monastery in Le Mans where she thought she was being led. However, on February 16, 1882, when she was attending Mass not far from the statue of Our Lady of Mount Carmel, she was overcome by the certainty that she was being called to the order of St. Teresa of Ávila. There was a recently founded Carmelite monastery in Lisieux where she had sometimes gone to pray with her father.

---

[271] Thérèse of Lisieux, "Poem to Mr. Martin," August 25, 1885.

Louis was alone in the belvedere when he saw his daughter coming to him, all excited. He welcomed her news with great kindness, allowing himself to ask only one common-sense question: Could Pauline's fragile health withstand the Carmelite discipline? Seeing his daughter's determination, he asked no other questions and gave her his blessing. But the father's heart was divided. On the one hand, he was deeply pleased that God was calling his daughter; it was a joy and an honor, and he knew he could count on the Lord to make his daughter happy. On the other hand, as someone who disliked separations, it was a deep suffering. He showed Pauline some of that emotion in the afternoon when he said that he was permitting her to enter Carmel for her happiness, but that it was a sacrifice on his part because he loved her so much. All the Martin girls would agree in considering Louis a modern Abraham. On October 2, 1882, the patriarch climbed Mount Carmel for the first time to offer a child to God.

It was with deep sorrow that he asked her as he left her there if he would ever see her again. At that point a grill separated visitors from the religious in Carmel, and the Martin family was permitted only a short visit once a week. But the parlors for visits soon became a great joy for Louis not only because he could be with his daughter again, but also because she introduced him to the great teachers of Carmel, John of the Cross and Teresa of Ávila. The humble father let his daughter teach him the paths of Carmelite prayer, and his soul, thirsty for God, was overjoyed by that.

But a new trial was waiting: Thérèse's health. Now ten years old, she was deeply shaken by the absence of Pauline, her second Maman, and this youngest daughter so loved by Louis fell seriously ill in March 1883. Medicine proved powerless, and Louis saw "my little Queen"[272] sink into sickness. She didn't recognize

---

[272] *CF* 221, 223, 228, 230.

him anymore, and one day he had to leave her room in tears because his child had cried out in fear at seeing him.

Louis, in his own words, stormed heaven to save Thérèse. Among other things, he had a novena of Masses said at Notre-Dame des Victoires. It was during his novena, on the day of Pentecost, that the family's well-loved statue of the Blessed Virgin came alive and smiled at the child, freeing her of all illness. It was with great joy that Louis wrote to one of his friends: "I tell you that Thérèse, my little Queen—that's what I call her because she is a lovely little girl—I assure you, has been completely healed. The numerous prayers have successfully stormed heaven, and God, who is so good, capitulated."[273]

Around this same time Marie met a great Jesuit preacher, Father Almire Pichon who, little by little, became the spiritual counselor for the whole family. Without Louis noticing it, his eldest daughter was beginning the difficult discernment that would lead her to Carmel as well. But before that, she allowed her father to fulfill one of his dreams: a pilgrimage to the Holy Land.

We know how much Louis loved pilgrimages. At the age of sixty-two, he was not afraid of the troubles along the way, just the opposite. Although he wouldn't end up reaching the Holy Land, during a month and a half he visited Munich, Vienna, Constantinople, Athens, Naples, and Rome, accompanied by a priest friend. His soul was flooded with grace over the marvels he encountered. He wrote to his daughters: "If I could make you feel everything I experienced in admiring the great and beautiful things that are unfolding before me! My God! Your works are so wonderful! . . . I could shout, 'It's too much, Lord! You are too good to me!'"[274]

---

[273] *CF* 220.
[274] *CF* 225.

Rome, in particular, touched his Christian heart. But Louis commented on his trip in Augustinian fashion: "All that I see is splendid, but it is a terrestrial beauty and our hearts are satisfied by nothing as long as we do not see the infinite beauty of God. Soon we will have the pleasure of being together as family, and it is this beauty that draws us closer to him."[275] Louis returned home joyfully with many stories to tell.

He could have finished out his life this way, surrounded by the affection of his daughters and as the beloved "king" of his domain at *Les Buissonnets*. When we consider the fruitfulness of Abraham's act of faith, which engendered a multitude of believers because he didn't refuse God his only son, one can imagine the fruitfulness of Louis Martin who offered God all his daughters, one after another, before offering himself, too.

The second of these sacrifices of a child, and not the least sacrifice, was Marie who decided in 1886 to join Pauline at Carmel. Louis had always loved his oldest daughter, "my diamond,"[276] in a special way, and this time he didn't succeed in concealing his pain. Marie said that he sighed in hearing the news. He was quite far from expecting it because there was nothing that would have led someone to believe she wanted to be a religious. As he choked back a sob and wondered aloud to her how he could ever live without her, she told him that Céline was old enough to replace her and that everything would be just fine. Her father then added that God could not have asked for a greater sacrifice from him. He had thought she would never leave him, and he embraced her to hide his emotion.

It was soon a double blow because during Marie's farewell trip to Alençon, Léonie, without telling anyone, entered the Poor Clares. The family was shocked, but Louis, with greatness of

---

soul, defended his daughter. He thought deep down that Léonie would not be able to keep the austere rule, but he supported her, and when she came back a month later after a dismal failure, he set about to soften her disappointment as best he could. He firmly believed that with the help of her mother, this daughter would also leave him for the cloister.[277]

On October 15, 1886, on the feast of Teresa of Ávila, Louis took Marie to Carmel. At Les Buissonnets, Céline, who was seventeen, took on the role of her big sister while Thérèse, now age thirteen, was burning with the desire to join her older sisters. After the grace of Thérèse's "complete conversion" that made her definitely leave childhood behind on Christmas 1886, she decided not to wait any longer and told Louis about her plan on the day of Pentecost 1887. Thérèse recounted the delicacy with which he received the news:

> Through my tears I confided to him my desire to enter Carmel, so then his tears began to mix with mine, but he did not say a word to turn me away from my vocation, being content simply to make me note that I was still quite young to take such a serious step. But I defended my case so well that Papa, with his simple and straightforward nature, was soon convinced that my desire was God's desire.
>
> In his profound faith he exclaimed that God was doing him a great honor to ask him for his children like this, and we continued our walk for a long time. My heart was comforted by the goodness with which my incomparable father had accepted the news, and so I poured

---

[277] Léonie entered different convents several times before finally ending up for good at the Visitation Monastery in Caen in 1899.

out my heart to him. Papa seemed to rejoice with the quiet joy that a sacrifice gives, once it has been made, and he talked to me like a saint.[278]

Louis then gave full rein to his paternal self-sacrifice. He didn't stop at giving Thérèse his permission, but after the refusal of the mother superior at Carmel to allow his daughter to enter at such a young age, he did all that he could to help her, with admirable disinterest on his part. He presented her to the bishop, he supported her, he comforted her, and, as a last resort, he took her to the pope in Rome to obtain the famous authorization! Monsignor Flavien Hugonin, the bishop they had visited, couldn't get over how eager the father was to give his child to God and how eager the child was to offer herself. Louis's zeal for God burned so strongly that he didn't consider his own pain, thereby making himself the perfect instrument of Providence. Without his support Thérèse wouldn't have been able to enter the Carmelites until she was twenty-one, so what would have ever become of her "running like a giant"?[279]

Because of the bishop's hesitation, Louis and Thérèse decided to go to the pope himself. They enlisted Céline—Léonie was gone, having entered the Visitation Monastery for the first time—to join them in the national pilgrimage to Rome. The great traveler Louis was quite happy to have the opportunity to show his daughters the beauties of Italy and the Eternal City. Louis experienced this new pilgrimage deeply, impressing the other pilgrims by his contemplative spirit, but also his exquisite charity. He left the best seats for others, he tried to cheer up a

---

[278] See *The Story of a Soul*, p. 108.

[279] A phrase Thérèse used to describe how she could move forward in the way of perfection after the grace of her "complete conversion" on Christmas 1866.

bitter neighbor, and he found an occasion to shake the hand of a pilgrim who had treated him like a Pharisee. He gladly took advantage of the time to be with Thérèse who was getting ready to leave him, not letting go of her arm. Louis was quite proud of his daughters, who felt the same way about him. "In the whole pilgrimage there was no one as handsome and distinguished as my beloved King,"[280] Thérèse wrote.

Then came the day for the papal audience. Thérèse received a prophetic word from the pope: "You will enter if God wills it."[281] And Louis, in a certain sense, received a prophetic gesture. After being presented to the pope as the father of two Carmelites, Pope Leo XIII, in a sign of special benediction, laid his hands on him for a long time. Marie, who was always close to her father in spite of the cloister, wrote to him that she was overwhelmed by the blessing of the Holy Father, but was not surprised that he gave him a special look. It seemed to her that the pope had blessed his white hair and his old age, and that it was Jesus himself who blessed him and looked at him.[282] Thérèse, a few years later with the benefit of hindsight, would see even more in the event: The pope had marked him "with a mysterious seal" in the name of Christ himself.[283]

Louis consoled his daughter for her apparent failure the best he could, but he shared her joy when finally, on January 1, 1888, she received authorization to enter Carmel. Three more months of delay were imposed on her, during which time Louis tried to heap every kindness on his youngest daughter, even proposing to take her to the Holy Land.

---

[280] *The Story of a Soul*, p. 124.

[281] Quoted in *LT* 36, Letter from Thérèse to Pauline Martin, November 20, 1887.

[282] See Letter from Marie Martin to her father, November 25, 1987.

[283] *The Story of a Soul*, p. 135

On April 9, he climbed Mount Carmel for the third time to offer God what was most precious to him. On his knees, in tears, he blessed Thérèse for the last time before seeing her disappear into the cloister. The next day he wrote a friend: "Thérèse, my little Queen, entered Carmel yesterday! Only God can demand such a sacrifice, but he is helping me powerfully so that in the midst of my tears my heart is overflowing with joy."[284] To someone who said that he could rival Abraham, Louis responded in a lively way that he would have to admit he would have slowly lifted his sword, hoping for an angel and a ram (see Gn 22). Céline described his paternal heroism at Carmel, and Pauline remarked, as Zélie's mouthpiece, that their mother had to be smiling down on him from on high and be rejoicing to see how he was steering his ship so well toward heaven.

Léonie was now back home, her first attempt at entering Visitation Monastery interrupted because of a health issue. Louis was confident that she would soon return. Only Céline, who was nineteen, was left. Seeing her talent for painting, Louis offered, a few months after Thérèse's departure, to accompany her to Paris to take some courses. Céline refused and felt obliged to share the reason with her father: She too had heard a call to Carmel. Louis invited her to go before the Blessed Sacrament to thank the Lord for the graces that he was giving the family, and the honor that he was showing Louis in choosing brides from his house. He felt that God was doing him a great honor in asking for all his children, and that if he had something better, he would hasten to offer it to him.

Even if the prospect of this new separation was painful, Louis was rejoicing. He was benefiting at this point from a particular grace of peace and joy. Behind the grills, he could sense the warm affection of his daughters. A supernatural joy filled him, and his daughters would consider this period as a kind of Ta-

---

[284] *CF* 230.

bor.[285] However, Thérèse would write:

> To live by love does not mean to
> Fix one's tent on earth at the top of Tabor.
> It means climbing Calvary with Jesus.
> It means considering the cross a treasure.[286]

Louis liked to recite the prayer that Marie had given him that accompanied a picture of Christ on the cross: "May everything be sacrificed to this cross. . . . And on the last day of my journey when death comes, may the image of the crucified God be found in me." After having offered God all his daughters, it was himself that Louis would offer as a sacrifice, becoming a living icon of the Holy Face.

One year earlier, on May 1, 1887, when he was almost sixty-four, he had the first attack of the illness that would eventually carry him off. When leaving for Mass at 7:00 a.m., Louis was struck by paralysis; all his left side went numb and his speech was slurred. It was the first attack of cerebral arteriosclerosis that would continue to develop in the next seven years with phases of remission and aggravation. It was associated with flare-ups of uremia, and it attacked his mental faculties.

For the moment, it would take more than this to prevent him from going to Mass. Like Zélie a few years earlier, he dragged himself there despite his problems, and returning home he told the girls that people are as fragile as the leaves on a tree because one night, like leaves, they look magnificent, but in the morning one hour of frost has withered them and brought them down.

---

[285] The site of the Transfiguration.
[286] *PN* 17, stanza 8.

Once he was alerted to the situation, Isidore prescribed total rest and came over to apply twelve leeches behind the ear of his brother-in-law, who had not lost his sense of humor, saying that the banquet table was quite small for so many guests. During the months that followed, Louis became more and more fatigued. On his pilgrimage to Rome, he became so pale at times that he frightened his daughters. In May 1888, after Céline shared her news, he went to Alençon. On his return, he recounted in the parlor at Carmel he had received such great graces and consolations in the Church of Notre-Dame that he told God the graces were too much and he was too happy. He thought he could not go to heaven like that and wanted to suffer something for God, so he had offered himself. Note that this occurred in Alençon close to where Zélie was buried, and it was in some way in following her example that he offered himself as "a living sacrifice, holy and acceptable to God" (Rom 12:1).

A few days later, the parish priest of the Cathedral of Lisieux issued an appeal to the parishioners. He needed 10,000 francs to construct a new main altar. 10,000 francs was the cost of a dowry for a Martin girl. Louis brought the money without delay to the astonished priest, asking only for anonymity. In learning about that, Isidore protested about a gesture he considered excessive. Thérèse commented that after having given all of his daughters to God, it was quite natural that he would offer himself to God too. The whole family seemed to foresee the Lord's response to Louis's gift-offering of himself.

Some people might believe in the piety of suffering for suffering's sake apart from the positive value of the cross. The cross of Christ saved us, however, and it is the same cross that every Christian, whose vocation it is to be an *alter Christus*, is called to embrace for the salvation of the world. Louis's sickness revealed a true passion whose complete fruit we will know only in heaven.

Louis's state became more aggravated toward the end of May 1888: illnesses, urinary problems, memory loss, disorientation of his sense of time, and similar problems. He became painfully aware of it himself the day that he found his favorite parakeet had died because he had forgotten to feed it. His daughters in the convent became alarmed at his condition, so Céline decided to stay close to her father as long as necessary. He was still peaceful, telling his Carmelite daughters not to be afraid of anything on his account because he was a friend of God. He wasn't waiting for God to extricate him from his dilemma, knowing that God would always do what was best for him. It was with full consciousness that he accepted the sacrifice and its consequences. One day when Céline had spoken to him about a man who had lost his mind, he had commented that in his opinion there was no greater trial than that.

His first hallucinations began in June 1888. Louis thought the lives of his daughters were in danger and that the war had returned. He even fled, explaining to his astounded daughters that it was so he could become a hermit. The months that followed were a nightmare for everyone. Often lucid, Louis at times prayed for death to come but always concluded, "All for the greater glory of God!"—a phrase he would repeat like a litany whenever he lost his footing. Céline testified that even when disjointed, all of her father's thoughts remained oriented to the service of God who had been the center of his whole life. Céline was brokenhearted to see her father in this state. Her sisters in the convent had the added suffering of their painful inability to help because of the cloister. They all lived in fear of a calamity.

In January 1889, however, Louis seemed better. As the fruit of a special grace, he was able to attend the investiture of his "little Queen" and share her joy. On that wonderful day when Louis led his youngest daughter to the altar according to the custom of the time, Thérèse witnessed her father's Palm Sunday.

One month later it was the beginning of the passion, for him and for the whole family. On February 12, a date that Thérèse with sublime faith listed as among the biggest days of grace in her life, Louis experienced a delirium that was much more intense than the preceding ones. He thought that the revolution was at the gates of the city, and he grabbed a gun to defend his Carmelite daughters. Céline and Léonie were the only ones who witnessed this atrocious scene and were not able to succeed in reasoning with him. Having been alerted ahead of time, Isidore saw himself obliged to make the decision that needed to be made. He had Louis confined to the *Bon Sauveur* (Good Savior) Asylum in Caen. Céline later said that she and Léonie kept silent the whole time because they were so crushed and broken.

"When you are old, you will stretch out your hands, and another will fasten your belt for you and carry you where you do not wish to go" (Jn 21:18). That is what the passion consisted in: humiliation added to the horror of the situation. Rumors in the city, and even at Carmel, quickly swirled around. People claimed that Louis's austerity led to his condition, or that he had syphilis, or that his daughters were responsible for his state because of the grief they caused in leaving him. However, what crushed the Martin daughters the most was to know that their father, their adored "king," was "with the insane" and being taken care of by strangers.

When Thérèse referred to the "great trial" of her life, she didn't speak of her dark night of faith but of her father's illness. It was a trial she used as a catalyst for an act of pure faith. She had formerly discovered the goodness of the Father in the face of her own father, and now she was recognizing the humiliated face of Christ in Louis's face. Through her father's passion, Thérèse discovered the passion of Jesus, in all his "insane" love for human beings. It was during this period that Thérèse of the Child

Jesus became Thérèse of the Child Jesus and the Holy Face.[287] She wrote: "Jesus is burning with love for us. . . . Look at his face worthy of adoration! . . . Look at his closed and lowered eyes! . . . Look at his wounds. . . . Look at Jesus' face. . . . There you will see how much he loves us."[288]

For the Martin daughters, the family was struck down like Job's family, but according to Thérèse it was a "blow of love."[289] Together they agreed to put up a bronze plaque in the chapel at Carmel under the image of the Holy Face, with the inscription, *Sit nomen Domini benedictum*. The Latin verse is from the end of a passage in Job that says, "Naked I came from my mother's womb, and naked I shall return; the LORD gave, and the LORD has taken away; *blessed be the name of the LORD*" (Jb 1:21). The first fruit of Louis's passion was without doubt this explosion of extraordinary faith in the hearts of his daughters, and without it Thérèse would not have been the saint that we know today.

Louis was in an asylum, but living in a psychiatric hospital is not an obstacle to holiness. Founded by Monsignor Pierre-Francois Jamet, the Bon Sauveur Asylum was not the hell that one could imagine. This was still the time of pioneering work in psychiatric hospitals in which the sick were treated very humanely by religious who felt called to that vocation. The patients' treatment consisted essentially in perfectly regular daily routines and in constantly being occupied. During the three years he spent there, Louis was intermittently lucid enough to understand, accept, and sanctify his trial.

Sister Costard, who took care of him in a special way, welcomed him and told him that he could be a valuable apostle for

---

[287] In 1895, the whole family, following Pauline, had joined the Archconfraternity of the Holy Face. In venerating Christ's disfigured face, they venerated his passion and thus the mystery of our salvation.

[288] *LT* 87, Letter from Thérèse to Céline Martin, April 4, 1889.

[289] *LT*, Letter from Thérèse to Céline Martin, July 14, 1889.

all the sick people around him. He answered: "That is true, but I would rather be an apostle elsewhere than here. But this is God's will! I think it is to knock down my pride."[290] Louis told the doctor: "I have always been used to giving orders, and now I am reduced to obeying them. It's hard, but I know why God gave me this trial: I have not had any humiliations in my life, and I needed one."[291]

And he would be an apostle first of all to the patients. Louis understood how to look beyond the masks of dementia into people's hearts to convert them. He refused the separate apartment he was offered so that he could live with the others, share with them the sweets he received from his daughters, and never stop preaching the love of God to them. He edified the personnel as well. According to Sister Costard: "Not only did he never complain, but he also found everything that we did for him very good. He was constantly making renunciations." Like the other nurses, she was amazed by his gentleness and often repeated, "There is something so venerable about him!"[292]

Of course, he also experienced times of agitation, confusion, and hallucinations when he needed to be taken aside and away from the others. And then there was one very bad moment of misunderstanding: Two lawyers, claiming to have come on behalf of his daughters, came to see Louis and tried to get him to renounce all his goods. Louis broke into tears because he felt his daughters were abandoning him and didn't trust him. Nothing could have been more bitter for him. Fortunately, Céline and Léonie who visited him every week reassured him that was not the case. These visits, along with the letters from Carmel full

---

[290] *LT*, Letter from Céline Martin to Marie, Pauline, and Thérèse, February 27, 1889.

[291] *LT*, Letter from Céline Martin to Marie, Pauline, and Thérèse, March 9, 1889.

[292] *LT*, Letter from Céline Martin to Marie, Pauline, and Thérèse, March 4, 1889.

of tenderness and encouragement, were his consolation. But he didn't rely on those. Learning one day that Léonie and Céline were on vacation with the Guérins, he was happy for them and wanted them to stay as long as Isidore thought necessary; he didn't want them to come back on his account.

His greatest support, as always, was prayer. He was the most constant visitor to the chapel and took Communion as often as his condition permitted. During his times of lucidity, he would discern God's will in the situation and pray to live in a holier way. When his daughters proposed a novena to ask for his healing, he responded that they shouldn't ask for that but instead should only ask for God's will. We can recognize in this sublime surrender the ongoing extension of all the successive surrenders of his life. Louis, even in terrible circumstances, valiantly continued traveling his road to holiness. "I really believe," Céline wrote to her sisters, "as time goes on, the more the expression on his face is peaceful and holy."[293] We only need to look at the last picture of Louis when he was alive to be convinced of that.

During those three years he weakened little by little, mentally and physically. In 1892, Céline described the result of his attacks as producing a childhood that was not quite childhood because he understood and felt more than children do; she could see the grief he was experiencing over not being able to express himself the way he wanted to.

Louis was no longer a danger to others or to himself, and his paralyzed legs reduced his autonomy, so he was released from the hospital on May 10, 1892. Two days later he was taken to Carmel. He wasn't able to speak, but he seemed to understand what his daughters said to him. And when they said goodbye, he managed to point his index finger upward and to articulate "in heaven." His return to the family softened the trial both

---

[293] *LT*, Letter from Céline Martin to Marie, Pauline, and Thérèse, May 20, 1890.

for him and for his children. Léonie and Céline rented a small house close to the Guérins in Lisieux and set their father up on the first floor. Désiré, a devoted maid, was hired to care for him. Because of her contact with the elderly saint and massive prayers by Céline, Désiré ended up being converted. The Guérins were always a valuable help, too, and watched over the whole family.

Louis was always gentle and sweet toward the family even if he sometimes seemed plunged into deep sadness. He rarely spoke, but never in a delirious way, showing his joy when Pauline was elected prioress at Carmel in 1893 or asking that they pray for him. In the midst of the diminishment of his faculties and his memory, certain personality traits remained intact: his gentleness and his contemplative soul. He was never happier than when outdoors in the countryside.

The Guérins had inherited a property near Evreux called La Musse, and Louis spent his last two summers there. Céline recounted a scene there in which he seemed better: "I will remember for the rest of my life his beautiful face when, as the sun was going down, we stopped deep in the forest to listen to a nightingale. He listened with such an expression on his face! It was like ecstasy, something inexplicable about the country that was reflected in his features. Then after a long moment of silence, since we were still listening, I saw tears streaming down his dear cheeks."[294]

Louis died at La Musse. On July 27, 1894, he was notably weakening, and on July 28 he received the Last Sacraments. His agony began on Sunday, July 29. He had difficulty breathing and seemed unconscious. But when Céline recited the invocation "Jesus, Mary, and Joseph" a little before 8:00 a.m., Louis opened his eyes wide and looked at his daughter with a tenderness she

---

[294] *LT*, Letter from Céline Martin to Marie, Pauline, and Thérèse, July 3, 1893.

would never forget. In his lively gaze she seemed to rediscover, for the space of an instant, her "king" in the splendor of earlier times. Then Louis closed his eyes forever. At the beginning of that Sunday, the Lord's Day that he had defended so much, Louis entered into Life.

On his mortuary card was this verse: "Was it not necessary that the Christ should suffer these things and enter into his glory?" (Lk 24:26). Heaven is never far away, and Thérèse sang of it: "Our dear father is near us! After a *death* for five years, what a joy to find him always the same, looking as he always did for ways to please us."[295] Louis was reunited with Zélie, his Hélène, his sons, and his first little Thérèse. He had to wait until 1959 for the death of Céline, who had also become a Carmelite, so that the whole family could be reunited at last.

Louis had said, about this family who showed the whole world the loving face of God, "I feel I must thank God and have you thank him too because I sense that our family, although humble, has the honor of being numbered among the privileged ones of our blessed Creator."[296]

---

[295] *LT*, 169. Letter from Thérèse to Céline Martin, August 19, 1894.
[296] *CF* 231.

Conclusion

CANONIZING SAINTS AS A COUPLE

Providence wanted us to wait one hundred fifty years after their marriage for Louis and Zélie, together as a couple, to be proclaimed blessed. However, the *vox populi* (voice of the people) of those close to them canonized them while they were living. The Martin daughters spoke of them only as their "saintly" parents, and Isidore considered himself a spiritual "pygmy" next to them. The neighbors, friends, priests, and religious in their circle all agreed about their holiness. The universal Church would not have known about them until later, in heaven, if their youngest daughter had not aimed a spotlight on her parents, whom she praised so often: "The good Lord has given me a father and a mother who are more worthy of heaven than of earth!"[297]

> Lift your eyes to the Holy Land
> And you will see on thrones of honor
> A beloved Father . . . a cherished Mother . . .
> To whom you owe your immense happiness![298]

On the evening of Thérèse's canonization on May 17, 1925, Cardinal Antonio Vico, who was responsible for the causes of beatification, said, "Well, now we are going to ask Rome to take

---

[297] *LT* 261, Letter from Thérèse to Abbot Bellière, July 26, 1897.
[298] *PN* 16, stanza 5.

care of the Papa!" The publication of the family correspondence, starting in 1941, brought Zélie out of the shadows. Father Stéphane-Joseph Piat then wrote *Histoire d'une famille* [*The Story of a Family*] a best-seller worldwide.

Since that time, Carmel and the Vatican have received thousands of letters from every country testifying to people's affection for Louis and Zélie, and to graces obtained through their intercession: healings, family reconciliations, conversions, temporal and spiritual graces. Louis and Zélie are not on vacation! Here are some examples sent to Céline from the United States in the 1950s:

> We would be very grateful if you would send us 1,000 pictures of Louis Martin and 1,000 of Zélie Martin with a prayer for their beatification. We can distribute them here and work for this holy cause. We believe they have already performed a miracle here in healing a little girl of the hopeless and incurable illness of blood cancer. A novena was said to them and she was healed. (From a prioress of a Carmelite Convent in the United States)

> The dear father [Louis] continues to practice his charity even on this continent. One example. One of our sisters, Sister Delphine, who is now deceased, received a visit from a mother who asked for counsel about the heavy cross she had to carry. Sister Delphine told her, "Pray to St. Thérèse." A few day later, this mother, in passing by the Franciscan Church of St. Peter in the heart of Chicago, met an old man who asked her, 'Are you troubled? Go into this church and at 3:00, when a tall man goes into the confessional, go tell him your troubles, and he will help you.' The young woman found the priest the gentleman had told her about, and he was able to strengthen

her fully. Her aunt was later showing her Father Piat's book *Histoire d'une âme*, and what a surprise it was for them in leafing through the pages to discover the picture of Mr. Martin. The young woman, exclaimed, "That's the same man I met in front of St. Peter's who told me to go in!' .... This is only one example. ... That beloved father is doing good on the earth along with his Thérèse." (From Sister Marie Stéphanie, United States)

I prayed to the mother and father of St. Thérèse, Louis and Zélie Martin, to help me save my home, because we were on the verge of divorce. I am happy to say that because of their intercession, my prayer was immediately granted." (From Mrs. J., United States)

The petitions asking for their beatification had tens of thousands of signatures. In response to popular sentiment, the bishops of Lisieux and Alençon opened up two processes for beatification that were first done separately from 1957 to 1960 and then joined into one single process. Father Simeon of the Holy Family, the postulator for the cause, Monsignor Giovanni Papa, and Mrs. Marie Perier furnished a historical and critical work that was considerable over the years. The *positio* (all the official documentation on the person's life and writings) was a dossier of more than 2,000 pages on all aspects of the Martins' lives.

For the first time, the cause of a couple was introduced at the Vatican. Different events would slow down the process, and it was not until 1994 that Pope John Paul II signed the "Decree of Heroic Virtues" for Louis and Zélie, proclaiming them "venerable."

Before beatifying or canonizing a person, the Church very prudently always asks for a confirmation from heaven, that is, a miracle. And one happened for an Italian family in June of 2001.

Valter and Adèle Schiliro had a baby boy named Pietro whose lungs were badly developed and who was surviving only because he was on a respirator. The doctors had called his case hopeless. On the advice of Father Antonio Sangalli,[299] the whole family, the personnel at the hospital, the parish, and prayer groups started praying to Louis and Zélie. Their answer was not long in coming. Pietro was soon completely and miraculously healed. Today he is a charming young man who comes to Lisieux with his family to thank his "parents in heaven."

At the end of a long and very detailed investigation, the Church recognized this healing as a miracle through the intercession of the Martins, and on July 13, 2008, exactly 150 years after the very day of their marriage, it was announced that their beatification would occur on October 19 of that year.

Those who participated will never forget that simple but grand ceremony in Lisieux with 15,000 joyful and fervent people from all around the world. If the reader will allow me to share a personal memory, that day was among the most beautiful I have ever known. Seeing the basilica decorated with colors and lights, filled with a crowd that was applauding, cheering, and singing heartily, I couldn't help but imagine Louis and Zélie in our midst, moved and almost astonished. Would these humble parents and humble workers ever have thought during their lifetime that the glory of the Church on earth—not to mention the Church in heaven—would be conferred on them? Zélie in particular would have probably been wide-eyed. This perhaps tells us something about the glory that is hidden in our humble daily lives, in our difficulties. "For this slight momentary affliction is preparing for us an eternal weight of glory beyond all comparison" (2 Cor 4:17). I felt I glimpsed the glory granted to the Martin

---

[299] Father Sangalli, O.C.D., has been a tireless vice-postulator for their cause.

couple that day, which is none other than the glory of God, and we shared in that time of grace.

Since then, the number of pilgrims who come to Lisieux or to Alençon has increased steadily. They testify that Louis and Zélie are by their side, especially in their family life. Parents grieving because of a child or because of a sickness experience the support of the Martins. Numerous couples who had not been able to have children have entrusted themselves to their intercession, and many little Louises and Zélies have been born. Since 2008 "Zélie" has been on the list of favorite names in France. For many people, Louis and Zélie are more than patron saints or even models: they are friends and even relatives. In a certain way, the Martin family continues to grow, added to by people that Louis, Zélie, Thérèse, and all the siblings welcome with open arms and surround with their solicitude.

The shrines at Lisieux and Alençon receive these kinds of testimonies every day, and we will hear wonderful stories later in heaven. The Martins don't solve everyone's problems, but with their daughter they could have promised, as she said: "Don't believe that when I am in heaven I will let ripe plums fall into your mouths. . . . That isn't what I had nor what I desired. You perhaps have great trials, but I'll send you great lights which will make you appreciate and love them. You will be obliged to say like me, 'Lord, You fill us with joy for all the things you do for us.'"[300]

The Martins' influence has been worldwide and pilgrims have come to Alençon from 110 different countries. Communities from around the world have put themselves under their patronage, like the important new community in Brazil, the *Sagrada Familia*. The Martin relics continue to be displayed on tour in various dioceses and, significantly, were present at the

---

[300] St. Thérèse of Lisieux, *Her Last Conversations*, trans. John Clark (Washington, DC: ICS Publications, 1977), p. 60.

Synod of Bishops on the Family in Rome in 2014. It was therefore appropriate that Louis and Zélie be canonized. If the beatification process holds up the Blesseds to be venerated in the local church (one reason why beatifications generally take place in dioceses), canonization holds them up to the whole Church.

Here again, there needed to be a miracle. On October 15, 2008, Carmen was born quite prematurely in Valencia, Spain. Complications quickly arose, and Carmen had a terrible cerebral hemorrhage. Her father asked for prayer at the nearby Carmelite Monastery. On November 23, when Carmen's condition was desperate, the prior of Carmel encouraged the parents to pray to Louis and Zélie. The next day, to everyone's surprise, Carmen began to improve, and at the beginning of 2009 she was able to go home.

But the cerebral hemorrhage persisted and had consequences that can be devastating. The Carmelites and the family, who went to see the relics of Louis and Zélie that were on tour in their area, initiated a new prayer offensive. On February 19, a medical exam showed the hemorrhage had disappeared and, even more improbable, there were no neurological or motor aftereffects. Carmen is a healthy little girl today.

Once her miracle was recognized on March 18, 2015, her parents said that the news about the canonization of Blessed Louis and Zélie Martin filled them with emotion, joy, and gratitude. They consider them part of their family, since they prayed to them and the Martins interceded for the healing of their daughter. The Martin couple, they said, is an example of a united family whose foundation is love and respect for children, so, thanks to them, they would be able to demonstrate those values to their two children.

Pope Paul VI said that if the Martins were canonized, they should be canonized together. He took the initiative to combine their two causes for beatification into one cause. The Holy

Father's action was powerful as well as innovative because the Church had never before proposed recognizing the sanctity of a couple. In canonizing a couple as a couple for the first time in its history, the Church is sending a powerful message, showing the beauty of God's plan for marriage and family and recalling that marriage is one of the royal paths to sanctification. Louis and Zélie had doubted that themselves, and it would be interesting to ask ourselves if, in our collective Catholic unconscious (if such a thing exists!), the idea still exists that sainthood is connected only to consecration or an extraordinary path.

The canonization of Louis and Zélie underscores that the family can be a place of love so strong that it testifies to the whole world of God's love and that an ordinary life lived with God can bear extraordinary fruit. By living this love in a simple way within the family every day, right to the end, Louis and Zélie participated in illuminating the whole world. Like their daughter, they are spending their time in heaven doing good on earth, and I encourage you to experience that yourself by entrusting yourself to them. You won't regret it.

Acknowledgments

If you liked this book, you can thank with me:

Monsignor Lagoutte, Rector Emeritus of the Sanctuary of Lisieux, for his preface;

Julie Romer and Claire Perot for their helpful corrections;

Sisters Alexandra and Marie Perier for their support;

Dominique Menvielle, who encouraged and guided me in my work.

Thank you from the bottom of my heart.

This book is a translation of *Louis et Zélie Martin: Les saints de l'ordinaire*, by Hélène Mongin, communications editor for Éditions de l'Emmanuel, located in Paris, France. She is also the editor of *Thérèse de Lisieux: Une pensée par jour*.